Geoglyphs
of the Desert Southwest

Earthen Art as Viewed from Above

Harry Casey | Anne Morgan

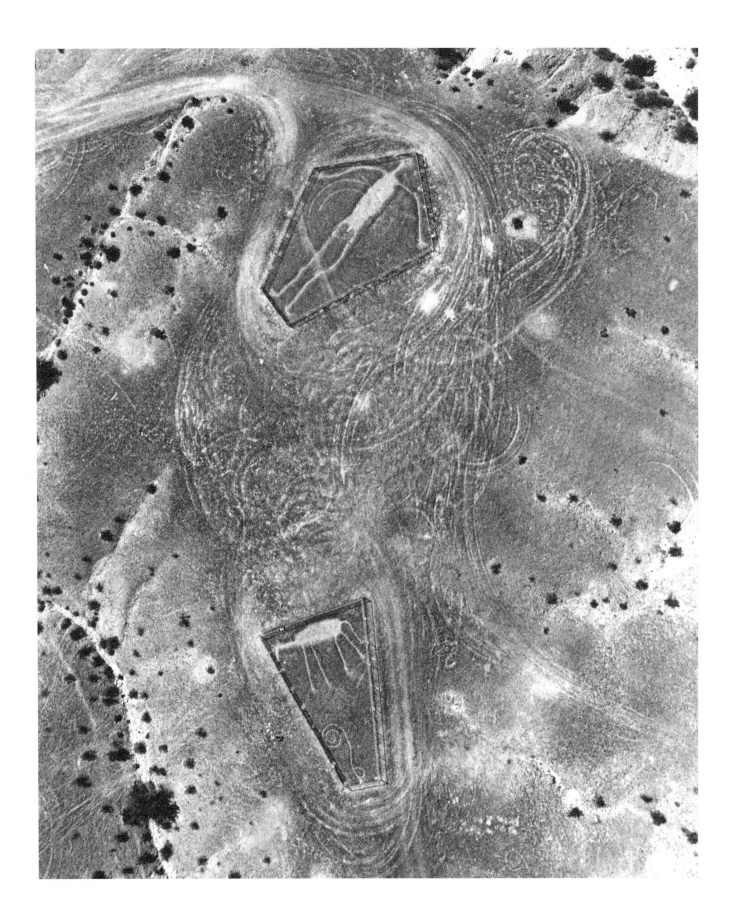

Geoglyphs
of the Desert Southwest
Earthen Art as Viewed from Above

Harry Casey | Anne Morgan

Sunbelt Publications, Inc.
El Cajon, California

Geoglyphs of the Desert Southwest: Earthen Art as Viewed from Above

Sunbelt Publications, Inc.
Copyright © 2019 by Harry Casey and Anne Morgan
All rights reserved. First edition 2019

Cover and book design by Kathleen Wise
Project management by Deborah Young
Printed in the United States of America

Sunbelt Publications, Inc.
P.O. Box 191126
San Diego, CA 92159-1126
(619) 258-4911, fax: (619) 258-4916
www.sunbeltpublications.com

22 21 20 19   4 3 2 1

Library of Congress Cataloging-in-Publication Data

Names: Casey, Harry, 1930- author. | Morgan, Anne, 1981- author.
Title: Geoglyphs of the desert Southwest : earthen art as viewed from above
/
  by Harry Casey and Anne Morgan.
Description: First edition. | San Diego, CA : Sunbelt Publications, Inc.,
  2019. | Includes bibliographical references and index.
Identifiers: LCCN 2018053990 | ISBN 9781941384503 (softcover : alk. paper)
Subjects: LCSH: Indians of North America--California--Antiquities--Aerial
  photographs. | Indians of North America--Arizona--Antiquities--Aerial
  photographs. | Geoglyphs--California--Aerial photographs. |
  Geoglyphs--Arizona--Aerial photographs. | Earthworks
  (Archaeology)--California. | Earthworks (Archaeology)--Arizona. |
  California--Antiquities--Aerial photographs. |
  Arizona--Antiquities--Aerial photographs. | Aerial photography in
  archaeology--California. | Aerial photography in archaeology--Arizona.
Classification: LCC E78.C15 C37 2019 | DDC 979.004/97--dc23 LC record
available at https://lccn.loc.gov/2018053990

All photographs are by Harry Casey unless noted.

"Mustamho stirred and compressed darkness to form sky and earth.

Male sky lay over female earth and offspring was…

Matavilla… Creator of Man."

—Mojave creation belief

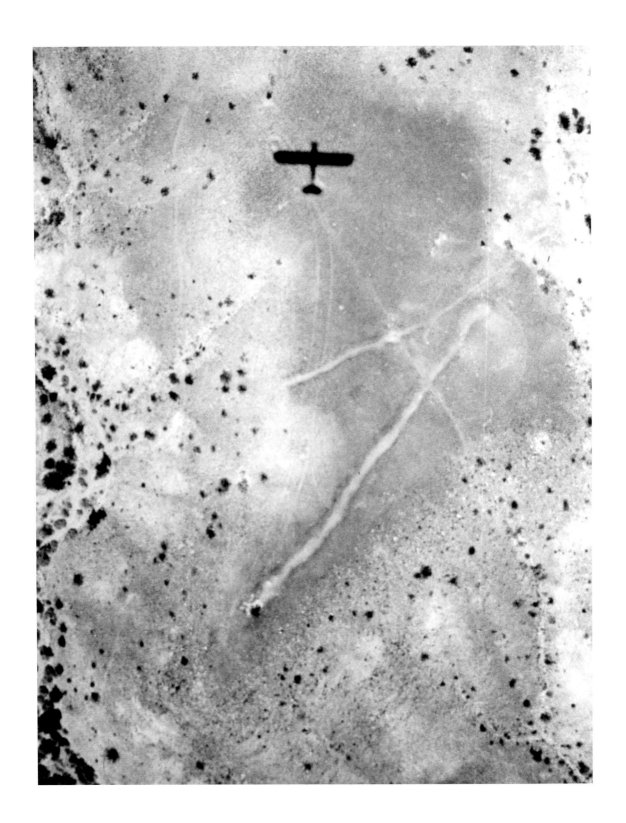

CONTENTS

Fisherman geoglyph.

INTRODUCTION

In 1976, Imperial Valley College archaeology professor Jay von Werlhof; Imperial Valley native, pilot, and photographer Harry Casey; and archaeology students from Imperial Valley College in El Centro, California, began a unique archaeological project: using aircraft to locate and photograph ancient ground drawings. This effort was to prove so successful that it escalated into the first major attempt to record earthen art sites in the deserts of the extreme southwestern United States.

This campaign began using 35 mm film cameras, aeronautical charts, 7.5- and 15-minute topographical maps, handheld magnetic compasses, and an antique 1946 Piper J3 "Cub" aircraft. This massive project had no sponsors or financial grants. The enthusiasm of the participants overcame formidable logistical and monetary problems to ensure detailed recordings were documented for future earthen art researchers.

There are more than 300 individual earthen art elements in the extreme southwestern United States: southeastern California and southwestern Arizona. A considerable amount of the fragile earthen art may not be discovered, recorded, and protected in time to prevent its loss.

Many of the geoglyphs located along the Colorado River are believed to be of significant spiritual importance to the Native Americans living in the area. Great care was taken to respect the sanctity of this fragile art during the photography project. The figures were treated with the same respect and dignity as any other religious sanctuary. Because of the fragility of these geoglyphs, and the potential religious and cultural significance of some, specific locations of geoglyphs are not provided in this publication. The intent here is to share the beauty of these amazing features, and open a new world to future generations whose privilege it will be to research and preserve this incredible ancient legacy.

ACKNOWLEDGMENTS

Encouragement and help have come from many friends and colleagues.

Boma Johnson, archaeologist with the United States Bureau of Land Management for over twenty-five years and a recognized authority on geoglyphs in the extreme southwestern United States, was particularly cooperative in sharing information concerning ethnographic data relative to geoglyphs located near the Colorado and Gila River areas.

This project would not have reached this degree of completion without the help of Imperial Valley College archaeology instructor Jay von Werlhof, who unselfishly guided and encouraged me in this lengthy photographic quest. His many contacts in the archaeological community proved to be an invaluable aid in gathering large quantities of previously recorded earthen art research material.

I am especially indebted to my wife, Margaret, who for the last thirty-five years accompanied me on most of the trips necessary to find, record, and photograph the widely scattered earthen art. She appears in several of the photographs, adding the element of human scale to these often massive works. As a retired high school English teacher, she was able to correct the many spelling and punctuation errors in this manuscript.

Finally, without the help of Anne Morgan, Archivist and Head Curator at the Imperial Valley Desert Museum, this book would not have been written. Anne became captivated by the project and volunteered to salvage my early manuscript, creating a more intelligible and coherent work.

The focus of this book is the photographs I have taken during the past thirty-five years, and my own small efforts at researching the geoglyphs in the region I call home. Unless otherwise stated, all opinions presented are my own. I hope this book and its photographs encourage a new generation of researchers to explore these little-known works and the ethnographic and cultural stories behind them.

Harry Casey
May 2015

ACKNOWLEDGMENTS

I would like to thank Harry and Meg Casey for their friendship and for sharing with me their experiences, stories, and knowledge of the deserts, geoglyphs, and rock alignments of Southern California and Arizona. And thank you, Harry, for trusting me to help see this project through to completion!

All my thanks and love to my parents: Kathy and Jim Morgan. Without your constant support and love, none of this would have been possible.

Thanks to the staff of the Imperial Valley Desert Museum for their help during my work on this project: Dr. Neal V. Hitch for his support; and Marcie Landeros, Angelina Amparo Coble, and Dr. David Breeckner for their help in ensuring all the photographs were digitized in a month-long project that probably taught them more about archives than they ever wanted to know.

The publication of this book would not have been possible without the financial assistance of the people who generously supported my GoFundMe publishing campaign:

Dan Armstrong
Richard and Jane Bailey
Michael Baksh and Tierra
    Environmental Services
Rosalind Bergeron
Maria and Steve Birdsall
Bruce and Wendy Burden
Sandy Colony
Rick Colman
James DEvelyn
Kathy Dickey
Martin and Mary Fitzurka

Norma Sierra Galindo
Suzanne Griset
Tom and Karen Gonzales
Mark Hanley
Anton and Jenna
    Hasenkampf
Edmund Haskins
John Kavanaugh
Dennis Kesden
Betsy Knaak and the
    Anza-Borrego Natural
    History Association

David Andy Lang
Mike and Tina Mitchell
Robert Mitchell
Ernest Muccini
John Morgan
Michael Nabholz
Evelyn Oehler
Elise O'Leary
Bill Pape
Michael Pape
Sheena Roper
Barbara Royce

David Royce
Marianne Royce
Jim Royle
Daniel Rubio
Richard Ryan
Samantha Scalabrino
Iingliana Tan
John Tinsley
Lidia Walker
Kate and George Willis

Anne Morgan
February 2018

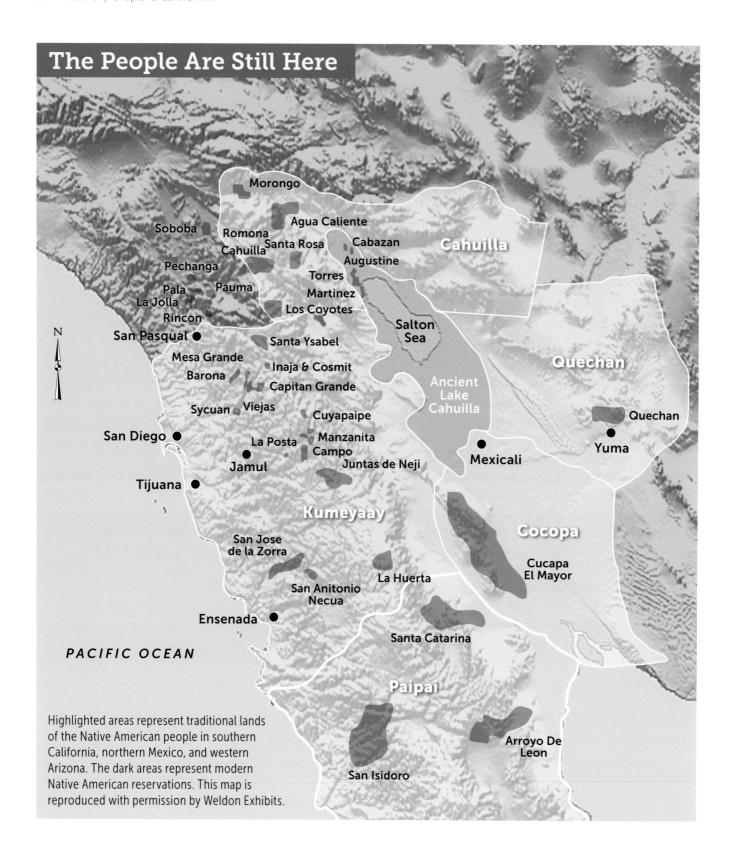

The People Are Still Here

Morongo

Agua Caliente

Soboba

Romona
Cahuilla   Santa Rosa   Cabazan

Pechanga   Augustine

Cahuilla

Pala   Pauma   Torres

La Jolla   Martinez

Rincon   Los Coyotes

San Pasqual   Santa Ysabel   Salton Sea

Mesa Grande   Inaja & Cosmit   **Quechan**

Barona   Capitan Grande

Sycuan   Viejas   Cuyapaipe   Ancient Lake Cahuilla   Quechan

San Diego   Manzanita   Yuma

La Posta   Campo   Mexicali

Jamul   Juntas de Neji

Tijuana   **Cocopa**

Kumeyaay   Cucapa El Mayor

San Jose de la Zorra

San Anitonio Necua   La Huerta

Ensenada

PACIFIC OCEAN   Santa Catarina

Paipai

Arroyo De Leon

Highlighted areas represent traditional lands of the Native American people in southern California, northern Mexico, and western Arizona. The dark areas represent modern Native American reservations. This map is reproduced with permission by Weldon Exhibits.

San Isidoro

N

PART 1
Chapter 1: EARTHEN ART

Throughout the deserts of the extreme southwestern United States are hundreds of mysterious ground drawings. They represent the almost-incomprehensible art form of ancient cultures. Ethnographic data has provided some clues but their origins, meanings, and purposes may never be fully understood.

"Earthen art" is a relatively new term for very old art forms. It has previously been called intaglios, geomorphs, stone arrangements, and petroforms. Now the more common expressions for the two types of earthen art are *geoglyph* and *rock alignment*. "Rock art" is the term used by archaeologists for pictographs (images painted on rocks) and petroglyphs (images "pecked" or carved into rocks). "Ground art" or "earthen art" is the term used by archaeologists for rock alignments and geoglyphs.

Rock Alignments

Rock alignments were constructed with locally available stones, arranged to create complex designs and long, sinuous lines. Occasionally gaps in an alignment were filled with gravel, which appears to have been scooped up by hand and deposited in the spaces. In some alignments, the stones touch one another. In others, the stones may be several feet apart. A few alignments were constructed with elongated rocks placed crosswise, touching one another in a way that

took considerably more effort to outline the design. One unusual alignment in the Mojave Desert features flat rocks leaning one against the other "domino style." Apparently, there was no common construction practice, as several adjacent alignments are often created using different methods.

Around the World

The ancient Australian aborigine and Native American could have had no cultural connection, yet both cultures created similar rock alignments. Fortunately, Australian aborigines still build stone arrangements. Thus, Australian ethnographic studies may provide some plausible motives for the construction of alignments in the southwestern United States.[1]

The meaning and function of Australian alignments varies considerably. Australian aborigines continue to use many of these alignments for a variety of ceremonies and initiations including circumcision, fertility rites, and rain-making rituals.[2] Alignments were also used to mark an important personal event such as a near-disaster to the artist or the killing of an unusually large game animal.

Australian researchers often separate the rock alignments into two categories: technological and demographic. Those considered technological are alignments used primarily for utilitarian purposes: fish traps, hunting blinds, shelters, and fire hearths. Those regarded as demographic are the alignments used for the various religious and mythological rites.

Geoglyphs

Geoglyphs were formed by the removal of portions of desert pavement in order to form an image. Desert pavement is the name given to the veneer of "closely packed pebbles, cobbles, and boulders that mantles a desert surface and overlies deposits of sand, silt, and clay."[3] Wind and rain have little erosive effect upon this stable surface. Desert pavement was the "blackboard" for the geoglyph artist. The pavement's dark veneer, called desert varnish, is a millimeter or thinner layer that covers the rock's surface. The varnish consists of about 60 percent clay minerals and 20–30 percent oxides of manganese and iron, as well as other compounds.[4] Desert varnish can provide archaeologists with a method of recording environmental changes and dating rocks (and therefore geoglyphs) with some level of accuracy.

The construction technique involved raking aside selected areas of the dark pavement to form a picture in the lighter subsoil. The pavement from the interior of the figure was heaped in a narrow mound, or "berm," around the silhouette of the image. This small berm of excavated material not only helped outline the figure, but also acted as a barrier sheltering the geoglyph against wind erosion. The desert pavement surrounding the geoglyph was never disturbed, as this provided the contrast enhancement necessary to create the silhouette.

Most geoglyphs were probably constructed using bare hands, stones, or wooden hoes or rakes to scrape away the surface gravel. Some of the lines may have been made by dragging or pushing a large stone to gouge a furrow in the desert pavement.

Occasionally, small designs or portions of a larger figure appear to have been "tamped-in" rather than cleared of surface gravel. Often the arms and legs of smaller stick-like figures appear to have been made in this manner. These tamped-in figures and their appendages were probably made by stamping the ground repeatedly by foot.

Many of the human-like figures constructed using this tamped-in method appear to be missing a head, arm, or leg. It is difficult to determine if this apparent omission was intentional or the result of deterioration caused by the less-than-permanent nature of the artwork itself. Tamped-in figures are usually small and indistinct when compared with those made using the scraping method of geoglyph construction.

Geoglyphs represent human (anthropomorphic) and animal (zoomorphic) subjects more often than do rock alignments. Geoglyphs are usually typical of other Great Basin rock art styles: humans are always portrayed as if viewed from the front, animals are drawn from the side, and reptiles are pictured as being seen from above.

Dimensions

The physical dimensions of earthen art are gigantic when compared to other kinds of rock art. Neither petroglyphs nor pictographs in our study area contain larger-than-life figures,[5] however, geoglyphs are anywhere from life-sized to as much as forty times larger than life. Geoglyphs and rock alignments vary dramatically in dimensions; some are less than three feet in size, while others can be at least 1,000 feet long.

Locations

Although geoglyphs and alignments are almost equal in number, their distribution is not uniform. Geoglyphs are usually situated on flat, dark areas of desert pavement near permanent water resources. Several anthropomorphic figures may be found perched precariously on the edge of a cliff, overlooking the Colorado River. Almost all anthropomorphic geoglyphs are positioned with their feet oriented toward the water, or at least in the direction of lower terrain. Most are found in a narrow band along the Colorado River, running from Yuma, Arizona, to slightly north of Needles, California.

Rock alignments do not share the geoglyphs' affinity for contemporary water resources, although many alignments are found around the edges of lakes that have been dry for thousands of years. These Pleistocene lakes occupied depressions in the Mojave and Colorado Deserts during a much wetter climatic period.

Alignments appear to be more widely scattered throughout the extreme southwestern United States and northern Mexico than geoglyphs and are also usually located at higher elevations. The alignments in the Mojave Desert are at elevations of between 1,000 and 4,000 feet. The few alignments along the Colorado and Gila Rivers are at the same elevations as the area's geoglyphs: generally less than 500 feet above sea level.

Age

Earthen art appears to vary dramatically in age. The youngest geoglyphs are about 300 years old while the oldest rock alignments may well be over 8,000 years old. Most geoglyphs appear to have been constructed within the last 1,500 years.

Dating earthen art has traditionally been very difficult. The age of a particular drawing is estimated by nearby tools, pottery, weathering, or the image content. The horse geoglyph shown on page 48 located near Yuma, Arizona, for example, is believed to be among the most recent geoglyphs. Horses were extinct in the Americas until their reintroduction by the Spanish in the 1500s, limiting the potential age of this specific geoglyph.

Since the early 1990s, a refined Carbon-14 dating method has been used to obtain dates for the construction of geoglyphs. This process involves using accelerator mass spectrometry (AMS) to date minute amounts of organic matter sealed under layers of desert varnish.[6] The process is based on the theory that subsurface rocks would only begin to be coated in desert varnish after being unearthed during the building of the geoglyph.[7,8]

An inherent limitation to any method of dating rock varnish is that the rock's surface must be exposed to the elements for varnish to begin forming. Therefore rock varnish can only be used to establish a minimum age.[9]

Geoglyph Dates in Southwestern United States
Through 1995

Geoglyph	Date by Accelerator Mass Spectrometry (AMC) ^{14}C	Estimated Margin of Error
Winterhaven Figure	840	± 25 years
Pilot Knob Anthropomorph	945	± 25 years
Blythe Anthropomorph (1)	1,060	± 65 years
Blythe Quadruped	1,145	± 65 years
Blythe Anthropomorph (2)	1,195	± 65 years
Ripley Anthropomorph	1,260	± 60 years
Quartzite Anthropomorph	1,380	± 25 years
Quartzite Amorphous Shape	1,480	± 25 years
Quartzite Anthropomorph*	1,540	± 25 years
Ripley lizard	1,560	± 40 years
Singer	1,600	± 25 years
Ocotillo snake	2,640	± 30 years
Schneider Dance Circle	2,790	± 25 years

*A second test was conducted on this figure. Ages differ by 180 years.

Dr. Ron Dorn, Professor at Arizona State University, Phoenix, developed the new Accelerator Mass Spectrometry (AMC ^{14}C) dating system used to date these geoglyphs.

Representation

What did earthen art represent to those who created them? Many geoglyphs appear to us to be nothing more than abstract symbols, but to their creators they may well have been as representational as the geoglyphs of human or animal figures. Rock alignments, which numerically represent almost half of the earthen art in our study area, are virtually indecipherable. There are only about seven or eight alignments that are indisputable representations of humans.

Around the World

Geoglyphs are not unique to the southwestern United States. Southern Peru and northern Chile have large quantities of this unusual art form, most famously the Nazca Lines in Peru. These images, which represent intricate, often stylized human and animal subjects, were constructed in a similar manner to those in California and Arizona. In southern Peru there are a wide assortment of geometric figures: triangles, rectangles, and trapezoids, as well as hundreds of perfectly straight lines,

many of which extend for miles. These linear creations required considerable engineering skill to construct, due to their straightness and tremendous lengths.

Further south, in the arid Atacama Desert of northern Chile, are more than 8,500 individual geoglyphs.[10] They are a highly diversified mix of human and animal representations, as well as geometric designs. The geoglyphs in Chile were constructed using two distinctly different techniques. One repositioned large, dark flagstones on a cleared surface to produce a positive dark image. The second, more widely used method, was to rake the darker surface gravel aside in order to expose the lighter subsoil. This process, called the "extractive building technique" by researchers in northern Chile, is similar to construction techniques used in southern Peru and the extreme southwestern United States.

Like geoglyphs in America, many of the famous Nazca Lines have been purposely damaged by vehicles, despite being registered as UNESCO World Heritage sites. Condor Geoglyph, Peru. 1988.

Chapter 2: **MEANINGS**

With little ethnographic evidence available, researchers have made little progress in their attempts to decipher the meaning of rock art. Most American rock art probably pertains to religious or ritual ceremonies or the recording of important historical or mythological events.

Ceremonies

Ceremonial dances are perhaps the most obvious reason for some of the oval or oblong geoglyphs along the Colorado and Gila Rivers.[11] Dancers following one pattern for an extended period of time would create elliptical dance patterns tamped into the ground.

There were dances celebrating the creation myth, for war preparations, or for rain and crop enhancement. Other dances were more social or personal, involving health, fertility, births, deaths, and coming-of-age rituals.

There are over forty circular dance patterns known to exist in southeastern California and southwestern Arizona. One of the most dramatic examples of the dance pattern is located along the Colorado River, where there are three dance circles of different sizes superimposed one on another. Ceremonial dance circles are often located near other types of geoglyphs. One of the giant human figures north of Blythe, California, has a large dance pattern overlaying the figure.

Such combinations suggest the anthropomorphic figure was the subject of a ceremony.

The evaporation of the Mojave Desert lakes 10,000 years ago meant that plants, animals, and humans had to adapt to new conditions or die. One theory suggests that the complex alignments in the Mojave Desert are the remnants of prayers for the restoration of more favorable environmental conditions.[12]

The Shaman

Shamans, as spiritual leaders, directed their people in rituals that may have included the construction of earthen art. Art was one method of divine travel, a vehicle to communicate with the spirit world. The shaman and his clan often journeyed to sacred ceremonial sites near the spirit world where the shaman would direct the group in ceremonial activities to engender blessings from the spirits. Areas more conducive to such pursuits were remote and often near prominent or unique geological features, which acted as aids in creating the desired psychological environment for the ceremony.

Celestial Observations

Celestial references appear in the ceremonies, art, myths, and songs of most Native American tribes.

Almost every Native American group in California observes both winter and summer solstices. Archaeo-astronomy research indicates the Anasazi and Hohokam peoples made solstice observations more than a thousand years ago and ethnographic evidence suggests that some geoglyphs were designed to reflect these celestial observations.[13]

The sun was believed to be able to bring rain or drought, light or darkness, heat or cold. The sun had powers of life and death over all earthly beings. The two extremes of the sun's travel (the solstices) were indicators of forthcoming seasonal changes and could be easily recorded with cairns, petroglyphs, or pictographs located where the rising sun would touch them only on the solstices or equinoxes. The comprehension of these events was of utmost importance in determining times to plant, harvest, and hunt, as well as for ceremonial and social functions.

There are very few homogeneous geoglyph sites. Therefore, when similarities are evident, they take on additional importance. There are six or seven figures on the west bank of the Colorado River that bear a striking likeness to one another. They all feature a large oval with a dissecting north-south line through the center of the oval. Additionally cairns, depressions, and other figures are arranged within each oval. Early studies of the "Black Point" site north of Blythe, California, led researchers to speculate that the north-south line might represent the Milky Way and that the position of the cairns and depressions could represent stars or constellations.

Territorial Claims

Geoglyphs can be found wherever there was a reliable source of water. This is particularly true along the entire lower Colorado River. Territorial claims may have prompted the construction of both forms of earthen art along certain sections of the river.[14]

Simple linear rock alignments, especially those of a more recent origin, appear to be territorial delineators. Several comparatively straight alignments along the lower Colorado and Gila Rivers may have defined property rights. These alignments are composed of widely spaced stones, not deeply embedded in the pavement, and are oriented roughly perpendicular to the river. It is as if the river formed the physical boundary and the alignment established the more political border.

Having delineated their territory, the alignment builders may have additionally protected their domain from the intrusion of enemies or strangers by posting graphic warnings. Some of the larger anthropomorphic geoglyphs may have been placed at strategic locations along important trails to intimidate trespassers. Their gigantic dimensions are inferences of ominous strength and power, which may have been calculated to strike terror into all intruders. As such, they may have been the original "no trespassing" signs.

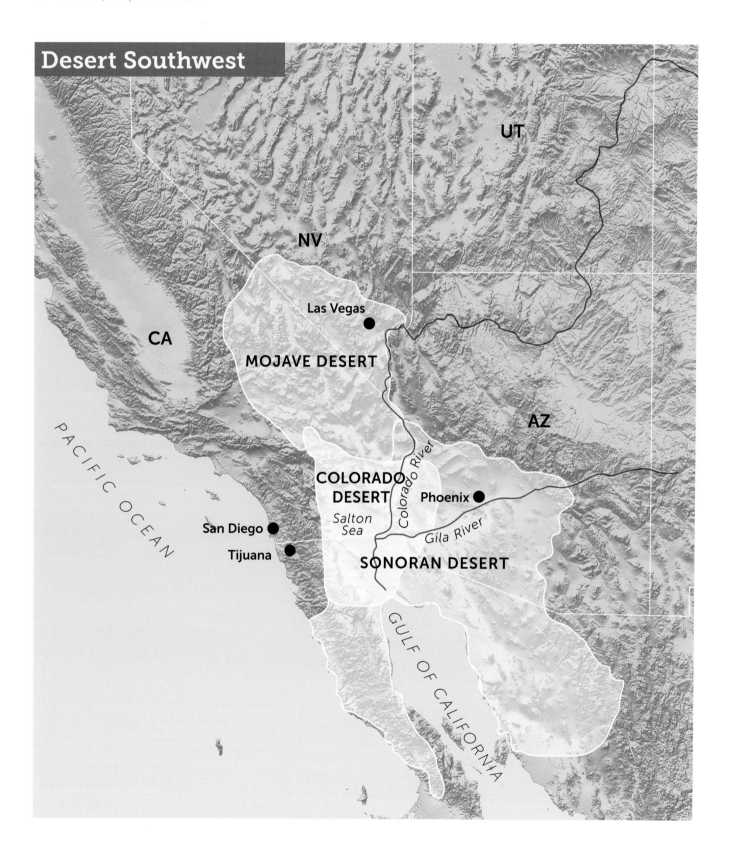

Desert Southwest

Chapter 3: **THE LAND**

Deserts

The desert is a paradox of nature: the extreme temperature, violent winds, and lack of rain tend to create an environment deceptively devoid of life, in which human survival is a never-ending struggle. Rainfall is not only scant but erratic, fluctuating from virtually nothing to as much as ten inches in an unusually wet year.

The earthen art described in this work is found within a geographic region that includes the Colorado and Yuha Desert regions of the Sonoran Desert and the Mojave Desert.

The Sonoran Desert

The Sonoran Desert is almost 100,000 square miles in size and includes the southern half of Arizona, southeastern California, the Baja California peninsula, and most of the Mexican state of Sonora. It is divided into subregions based on elevation and aridity. Its western subregion, called the Colorado Desert or Lower Colorado River Valley, is roughly 7 million acres from the Colorado River to the Laguna Mountain range and over 500 miles south into Mexico. A subregion of the Colorado Desert is the Yuha Desert in the Imperial Valley, California.[15]

The Mojave Desert

The Mojave Desert is nearly 48,000 square miles of high desert covering southeastern to central California, northwest of the Colorado Desert, as well as portions of Arizona, Utah, and Nevada. Within it are numerous rock alignments along the eastern perimeters of the long-dry Pleistocene lakes.

Rivers

The Colorado River

The Colorado River is the main river of the southwestern United States and northern Mexico. At 1,450 miles long, it is responsible for much of the formation of the landscape of the Southwest, including ancient Lake Cahuilla and the modern-day Salton Sea in California. Many geoglyphs can be found along its terraces, proof that it was a very populated area for thousands of years.

The Gila River

The Gila River is a 649-mile tributary of the Colorado River, beginning in New Mexico and extending across Arizona. Like the Colorado, it has been the focus of Native American habitation in the area since people first entered the region.

These two waterways are of vital importance in our earthen art discussion, since approximately 90 percent of the geoglyphs are either adjacent to, or very close to, these two river systems. On the other hand, only about 10 percent of the rock alignments are anywhere close to these river systems.

The main concentration of geoglyphs are located in a 165-mile-long band along the Colorado River, running from just north of Needles, California, south to Yuma, Arizona.

Lakes

Lakes of the Colorado Desert

For at least the last 27,000 years, and probably longer, the Colorado River periodically overflowed and changed course, filling the Imperial Valley and creating one of the largest freshwater lakes in North America: Lake Cahuilla. In the last thousand years alone, geologists believe that Lake Cahuilla filled and receded at least four times. At its full size, Lake Cahuilla was 114 miles long, 33 miles wide, and 315 feet deep.[16] It supported abundant plant and animal life, and Native Americans migrated through the area, setting up camps and villages along its shoreline. Presently all that remains of this lake is the Salton Sea, which (as of 2016) is 35 miles long by 15 miles wide and 44 feet deep.[17]

Lakes of the Mojave Desert

During the Pleistocene Epoch, lakes throughout the Mojave maintained a relatively constant water level, due to abundant rainfall and a lake-to-lake drainage pattern. These included Lake Manly, Panamint, Manix, Harper, and Owens Lake. These stable lakes provided the equilibrium necessary for thousands of years of human habitation. The gradual but dramatic weather changes at the end of the Pleistocene Epoch (8,000–10,000 years ago) had catastrophic results upon the people living in the area. The Great Drought (during the middle Holocene Epoch, about 6,000 years ago[18]) initiated the gradual change of the lush environment into the hot, dry desert we know today.

Chapter 4: **SUMMARY**

Contemporary man's fascination with rock art has only been heightened by his apparent inability to decipher its meanings.

The elders of most contemporary Native American groups often say that the figure, or at least its location, is of religious importance to them today. Weldon Johnson (Mojave) stated in a presentation, "To the Indians of the lower Colorado River, the Quechan, the Mojave, and the Cocopah, the giant figures are not something of the past, but are a part of the spiritual life of the Colorado River Indian today.... They are our sacred objects, held with the same respect as the giant Buddha statues in the Orient or statues in the Catholic Church."[19]

Ethnographic sources indicate that some elements were constructed to serve as pictorial records of important mythological events, while others were to serve as the nucleus for a variety of ceremonies. Many of these rituals were attempts to communicate with powers far stronger than those of man. These powers were believed to control the weather, plants, animals, and man. The shaman who acted as the liaison between man and these powerful forces was probably instrumental in their construction.

It is especially difficult to suggest motives for the construction of rock alignments. Most alignment studies in this country have not provided acceptable explanations for the existence of many of the rock alignments. They may have been esoteric sites, whose mystic alignment language was understood only by the religious leaders, who directed their construction.

The building of earthen art, especially the rock alignment, may have been a religious rite in itself; wherein the physical actions of making the design fulfilled the prayer or communication needs of the builders and the permanence of the created figure was actually of little or no consequence.

Ethnographic findings suggest rock art, especially earthen art, is located on what the Native American artist believed was sacred ground. Therefore, we should treat all forms of rock art with the same respect, dignity, and sanctity we afford modern religious expressions.

Individuals vested with the responsibility of rock art preservation have feared that public disclosure of the quantity of earthen art and its locations would hasten its demise. The Bureau of Land Management, in cooperation with the tribes, has fenced many of the more vulnerable geoglyphs. Even so, much earthen art has no or inadequate protection. The current unprecedented interest in desert conservation and cultural history may help focus attention on the need for more extensive earthen art research and preservation. Prospective global studies may assist in explaining reasons for the existence of some of the more enigmatic elements found here and abroad.[20]

Colorado River from Piper Cub plane window.

PART 2
PHOTOGRAPHS

The following photographs were taken during a thirty-five year period in an attempt to document the geoglyphs of the extreme southwestern United States and their changes (both natural and those caused by humans) over time. The names used for geoglyph identification are modern names based on their appearance, location, or the modern archaeologist who recorded them. Specific locations of geoglyphs, unless previously published by the Bureau of Land Management, are not provided in order to preserve these delicate sites.

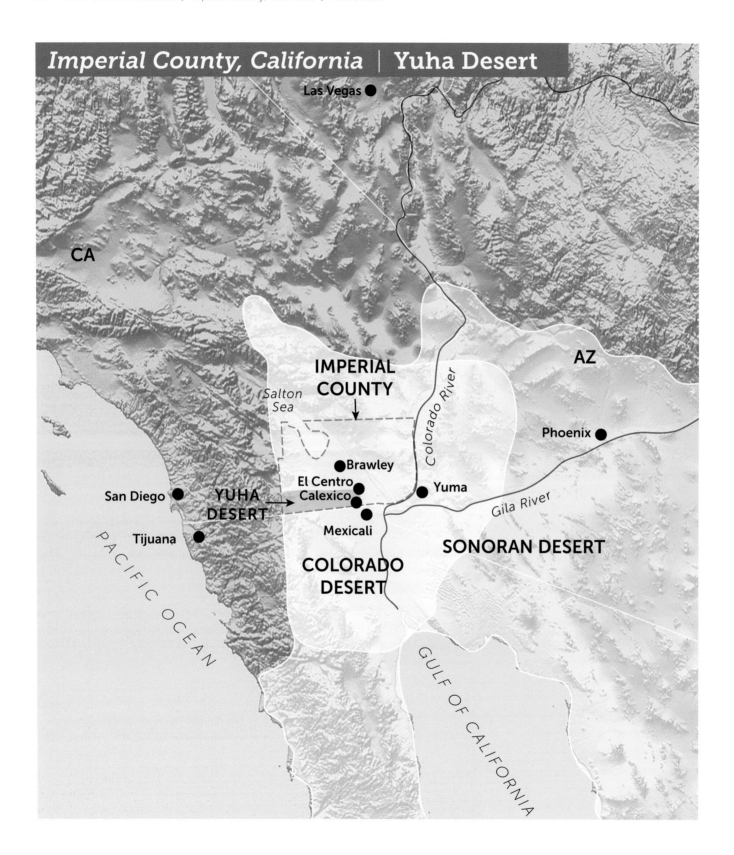

Imperial County, California | **Yuha Desert**

Imperial County, California
Yuha Desert

The Yuha Desert is a distinct section of the larger Sonoran Desert. Located in the Imperial Valley, California, it stretches west of El Centro and north of California's international border with Mexico. Once a lush, hospitable landscape, today it is one of the hottest places in North America and receives an average of under three inches of rain a year. The desert pavement here is lighter in color and not as enduring as pavement elsewhere, making the longevity of geoglyphs here less common.

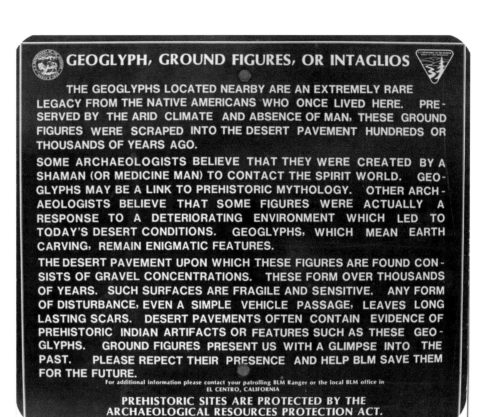

"Yuha Geoglyph"

The curvilinear and rectangular designs of this geoglyph, the largest of the three main Yuha Desert sites, have more intricate patterns than any other abstract ground drawings found in the American Southwest. The meaning of these symbols is now unknown, but may refer to territory boundaries, dances, or ceremonial rituals.

The desert pavement at this site is easily disturbed, since the small surface gravel is not firmly bound into pavement. The site was seriously damaged by vandals riding motorcycles in 1975. Using early aerial photographs and archaeological line surveys, the geoglyph was restored in 1981 under the direction of Jay von Werlhof, then director of the Imperial Valley College Barker Museum. It has been fenced off by the Bureau of Land Management to prevent additional vehicular damage.

Meg Casey at "Yuha Geoglyph" for scale. March 31, 1990.

Signage by the Bureau of Land Management. "Yuha Geoglyph."

Close-up view. "Yuha Geoglyph." March 1979.

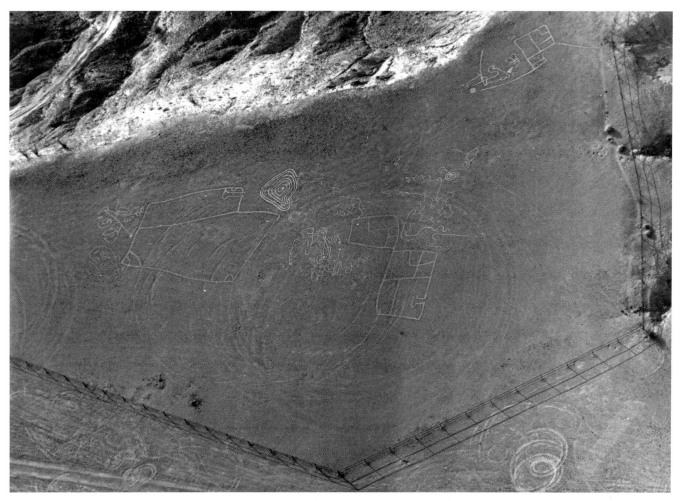

Damage from tire markings by motorcycle-riding vandals is visible across the entire site. "Yuha Geoglyph." March 1979.

Close-up view. "Yuha Geoglyph."

Close-up view. "Yuha Geoglyph."

"Power Circle Geoglyph"

This geoglyph, not recorded until 1979, is located about a half mile north of the "Yuha Geoglyph" site. The two large concentric circles are connected by a long meandering line, which runs south for about 550 feet. Along this line are two smaller circles four and six feet in diameter. The larger circle is attached to the wandering line by a three-foot path. The other circle is close to the line, but not attached. Within the double circles are a group of quartz stones arranged in a circle. Within this circle are two larger stones, one of which is elongated and set on end.

This site was interpreted in 1989 by Tom Lucas, the last Kwaaymii Elder. He said, "The land outside the outer circle represented the power all things possess, the power that enables earthly existence. The power within the outer circle was stronger and was accessible to humans through prayer or spiritual quests. None but a shaman could set foot in the power-laden inner circle. At its center, a hub of quartz cobbles evoked the essence of a world forfeit to shamans upon the mythic demise of their creator god."[21]

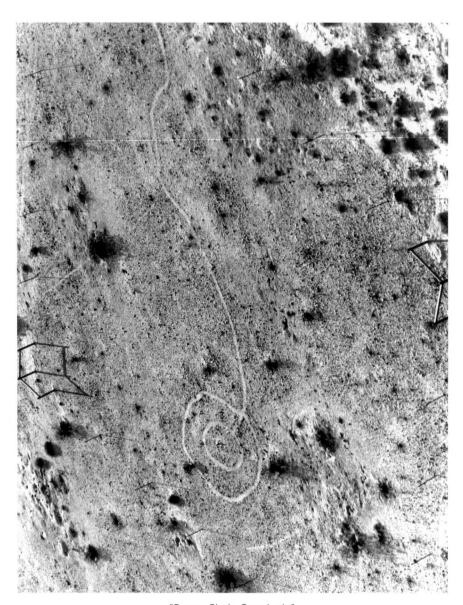

"Power Circle Geoglyph."

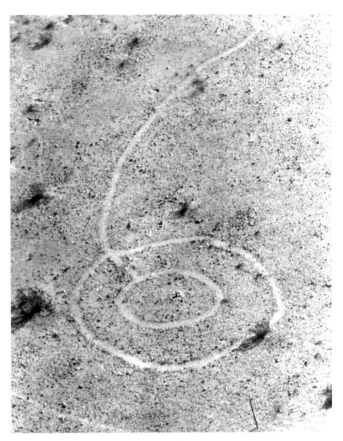

"Power Circle Geoglyph."

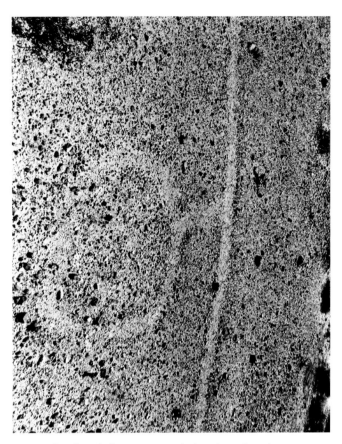

Smaller circles on a meandering three-foot-long path-like connection. "Power Circle Geoglyph."

Meg Casey for scale. "Power Circle Geoglyph."

"Schneider Geoglyph"

Portions of this geoglyph resemble a half dozen others found along the Colorado River. They all have a characteristic oblong circle, with a north-south line bisecting the center of the elliptical circle. This glyph is distinctive for its four leg-like appendages sloping down from the oval. In 2013, this site was interpreted by Steve Lucas, a Kwaaymii and relation of Tom Lucas, as representing the Milky Way.[22] The dance circle around it is, according to Lucas, the largest dance circle west of the Colorado River. It acts, he says, as the "frame" for the figure. This is the oldest of all known geoglyphs. It was dated by Dr. Ron Dorn of Arizona State University in 1995 as being 2,790 years old.

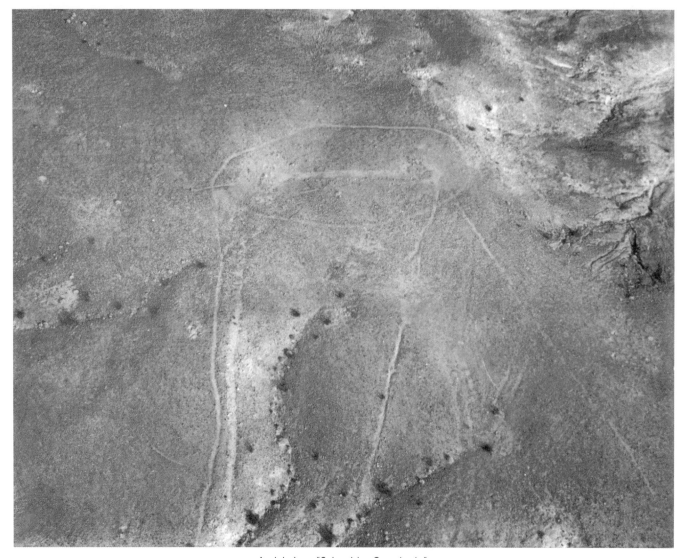

Aerial view. "Schneider Geoglyph."

"Nessie"

This particular site, sometimes referred to as "Nessie,"
is composed of two parallel
lines, one of which becomes
an undulating wave about
halfway across the alluvial
fan. It is located less than two
miles northwest of the "Singer
Geoglyph" complex in an area
known to have been heavily
used for training maneuvers
during World War II.

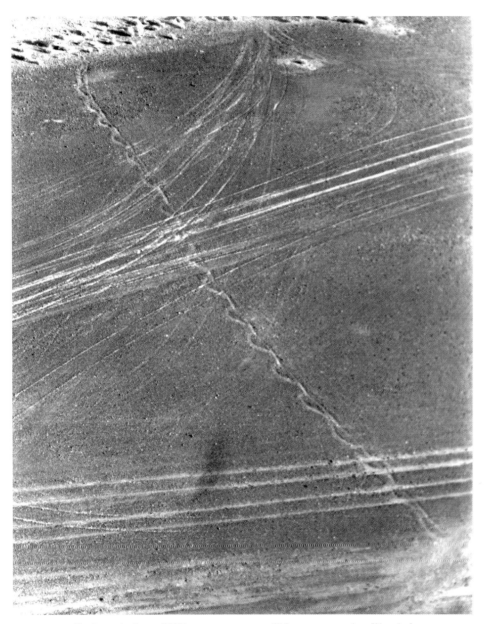

Tank tracks from WWII maneuvers can still be seen crossing "Nessie."

"Singer Geoglyphs" Complex

Originally called the "Gold Basin Rand/Intaglios," the current name for this site is the "Singer Geoglyphs." Prior to the opening of the Goldfield Mining Company's Mesquite Operation a few miles north of these geoglyphs, considerable environmental impact work was undertaken. This included a thorough surface archaeological study and extensive aerial reconnaissance, which revealed many geoglyphs. Using the AMS ^{14}C dating process in 1995, Dr. Ron Dorn determined that some of these geoglyphs were constructed as long as 1,600 years ago.

This geoglyph site is located 22 miles northwest of the large Camp Pilot Knob base, which was active between 1940 and 1942. Here the 6th and 85th Infantry divisions trained under the command of General George S. Patton. The remains of several smaller, temporary, military bivouac areas can still be seen, making it difficult to tell whether some of the features in this site are military marks instead of ancient geoglyphs.[23]

The "Singer Geoglyphs" are widely scattered over almost one square mile. All appear to be about the same age and have similar path-like meandering bodies. Occasionally, short, yard-long protrusions leave the main body only to terminate with a slightly widened area. Some of the figures appear to have been physically connected to others by a lesser path, which is now almost indiscernible. Unfortunately, a road was graded through the area and several of the geoglyphs were damaged.

The most easterly of all the Singer Geoglyphs, this is unique in that larger rocks appear to have been incorporated into the original design. Water erosion in the nearby wash may have disturbed a portion of the design.

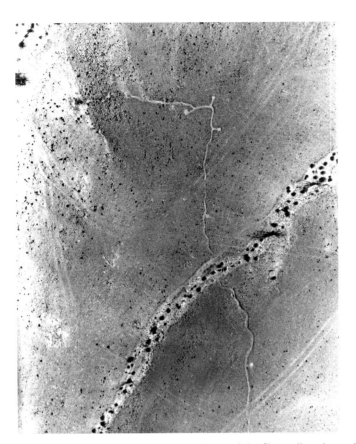
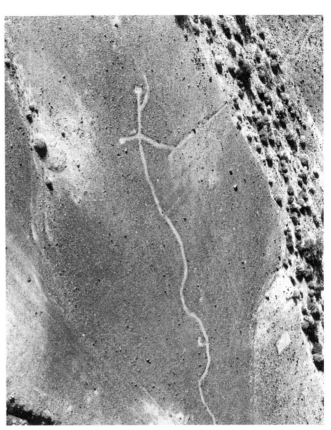

Many of the Singer lines have short, two-to-three-foot paths
leaving the main body only to terminate abruptly in a widened area.

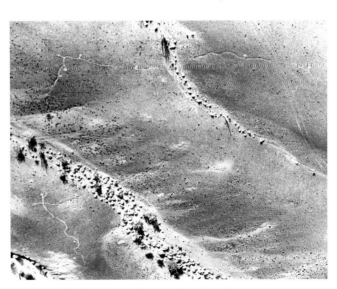

A road was graded through this area and several of the
geoglyphs were damaged. "Singer Geoglyph Complex."

Partial view of "Singer Geoglyph Complex."

"Quail Geoglyph"

The "Quail Geoglyph" is situated north of the World War II Camp Pilot Knob. It was constructed by pulling the surface cobbles to one side, leaving a lighter-colored sandy area. This was not the usual practice of the Native American geoglyph artists, who almost always raked the gravel equally to both sides, forming two berms of excavated material. This fact, the location, and the apparent newness of the glyph cast serious doubts about its authenticity as an ancient or historic geoglyph.

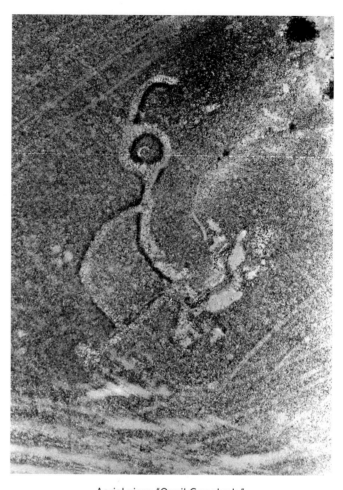

Two archaeologists recording geoglyph for scale.
"Quail Geoglyph."

Aerial view. "Quail Geoglyph."

"9-Point Star Geoglyph"

Researchers question the authenticity of this particular geoglyph for several reasons. First, it does not appear to be very old, and its precise geometric design is unlike that of any other "authentic" geoglyph. This star-like geoglyph is probably not the product of ancient Native Americans.

"9-Point Star Geoglyph." July 1985.

"Spoke Wheel Rock Alignment"

Listed on the National Register of Historic Places:
September 29, 2003

Early in 1994, a very unusual alignment was discovered west of the small town of Ocotillo, California. The design is similar to "medicine wheels" found in South Dakota, Wyoming, and Montana. However, this is the first "medicine wheel" alignment to be found in our study area. Located in an area of intense outdoor activities, shortly after its discovery the alignment was modified by unknown individuals. This site desecration upset many and prompted a restoration effort that included a local Native American elder who, using appropriate purification rituals, attempted to regenerate the site. Many Native Americans who have visited the location before and after the alteration say the site is now "dead" despite these efforts.

Pottery sherds were present in and around this site. This is unusual, as earthen art sites in our study area rarely have any cultural material nearby. The authenticity of recent discoveries such as this must be scrutinized with extreme care.

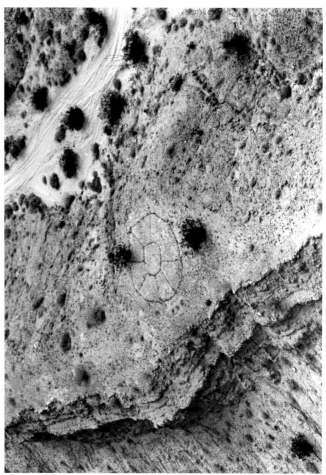

"Spoke Wheel Rock Alignment." May 1994.

This photograph shows the changes that were made to the original design. An inner circle and arrow-like symbol were added to the existing design using stones collected from the immediate area. Additionally, small white quartz rocks were deposited in a pile forming a cairn in the center of the new inner circle.

Parallel Rock Alignment

These rock patterns are unusual not only because they are located far from any other known rock alignments, but also because they consist of three roughly parallel lines of stones. Each row is spaced differently. The stones in one row are about four feet apart, while the other two lines average eight and sixteen feet apart. This triple alignment extends for almost 1,000 feet across several alluvial fans and is interrupted on three occasions by small ravines. This uncommon alignment is located northeast of the "Singer Geoglyphs."

Parallel Rock Alignment, Imperial Valley, California.

Mottled Areas

These unusual mottled (variegated, or spotted) areas are often found in the vicinity of geoglyph concentrations, and/or trail systems. It is possible that these depressions are simply a resting place for weary travelers and the items they may have been transporting.

This site in the western Yuha Desert has many small, cleared "mottled" areas.

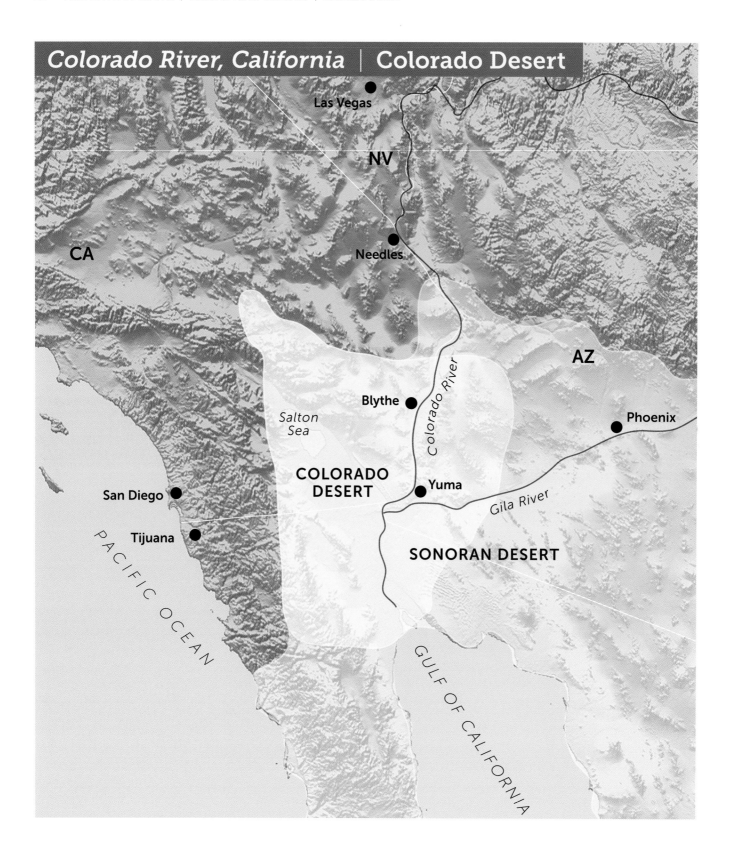

Colorado River, California | Colorado Desert

Las Vegas

NV

CA

Needles

AZ

Salton Sea

Blythe

Colorado River

Phoenix

COLORADO DESERT

Yuma

Gila River

San Diego

Tijuana

SONORAN DESERT

PACIFIC OCEAN

GULF OF CALIFORNIA

Colorado River, California
Colorado Desert

Blythe Geoglyph Complex

Listed in the National Register of Historic Places:
August 22, 1975

The "Blythe Giants" are easy to find and relatively safe for public scrutiny. They are the largest and most well known of all the Southwestern geoglyphs and have been restored, securely fenced, and given interpretive signage by the US Bureau of Land Management.

Located on a flat, gravel-covered terrace 12 miles north of Blythe, California, the site includes three humanoid figures, two four-legged animals, and one spiral design or coiled snake. The height of the humanoid figures in particular is gigantic: 176, 105, and 92 feet. Three of these geoglyphs (two of the humanoid giants and one of the quadrupeds) were dated by

Bureau of Land Management sign.
Blythe Geoglyph Complex. July 1988.

Dr. Ron Dorn in 1995 to 1,060, 1,195, and 1,145 years ago, a 135-year time span that suggests the Blythe area remained a significant location for generations of Native Americans.

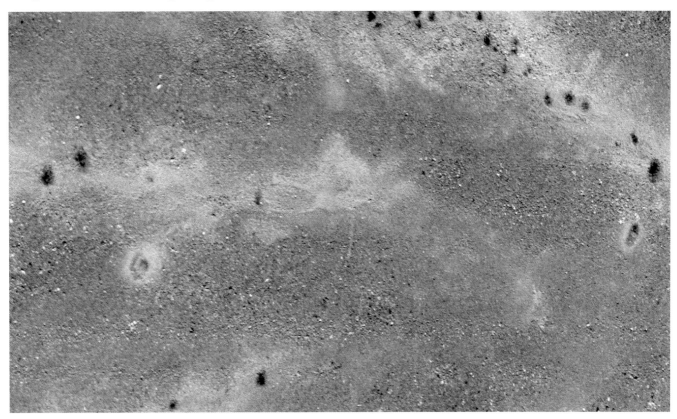

One anthropomorphic figure north of Blythe escaped the 1957 restoration efforts. October 1991.

The site was first recorded in 1932 by pilot George Palmer. His photographs led Arthur Woodward, Curator of History and Anthropology at the Natural History Museum of Los Angeles County, to conduct the area's first ground survey.[24] It was surveyed again in 1939 by archaeologist Malcolm Rogers.[25] Vandalism endangered the images and in 1957, De Weese W. Stevens, vice-principal of Palo Verde High School in Blythe, worked to have them restored by a group of student volunteers.[26] Although the work made the figures easier to see, and was based on the original 1932 aerial photographs, some changes were made by the students. Early photographs show that the original builders oriented the giant's right foot outward, like the knee, and the figure had the correct number of fingers and toes, something that was not done during the restoration.

One figure escaped the restoration efforts that made the rest of the effigies so easily seen. The lone figure is similar to the nearby Blythe humanoid figures, although it is only 35 feet tall, considerably smaller than any of the other humanoid images found near Blythe.

Boma Johnson connected these geoglyphs to oral mythologies of the Mojave, Quechan, and Hopi peoples. A Mojave story describes how one of the figures was made to represent Mustamho, the Creator God, in order to help them get rid of an evil giant who lived on the east side of the Colorado River and had, for many years, tormented the Mojave living in the area. Once the geoglyph was finished, they had a ceremony, dancing for three days and nights to gain the courage needed to kill the evil giant. A slightly different Quechan myth calls the evil giant Kwa-You. The tribes

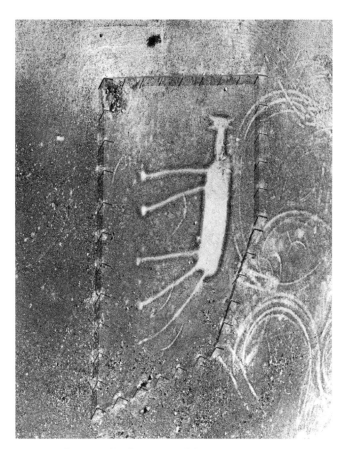

Zoomorphic figure, possibly a mountain lion. Blythe Geoglyph Complex.

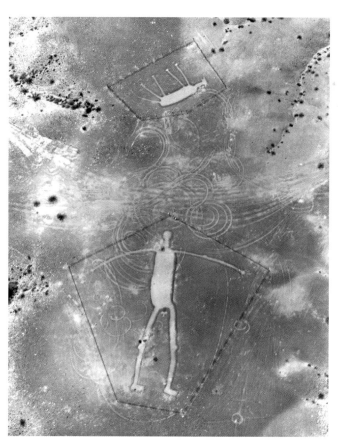

One set of fenced Blythe geoglyphs, anthropomorphic and zoomorphic figures.

asked for help from the Sea God, who sent a giant octopus up the Colorado River from the Gulf of California. The octopus and the giant fought, and the octopus was able to drag the giant into the river and drown him.[27] The octopus carried the giant's body back down the river, occasionally holding it up for people to see. Those who witnessed the event celebrated the giant's death by building effigies of the monster next to the river.

A Hopi legend states that several Hopi clans migrated south from Utah to the Blythe-Parker area, where two of the clans fought. The victors (the Fire Clan) made a giant effigy of their clan deity on order to keep the other clan from returning.[28]

Other stories describe one of the giants and the animal (here a mountain lion) as a way of telling a creation story. The animal figures represent Hatakulya, one of two mountain lions/people who helped Mustahmo in the Creation of Life. Ceremonial dances were held in the area to honor the Creator of Life.[29] Kumastamxo/Mustamho "created the sun and stars and offered seeds to the progenitors of the tribes of the Quechan, the Kumeyaay, and the Maricopa. And close by he was attended by a first shaman, a mountain lion, for back then, animals could be shamans."[30] The spiral design in this story is said to represent the Colorado River and "upon Kumastamxo striking the ground with his spear, its water poured forth. With his spear, he marked its winding course."[31]

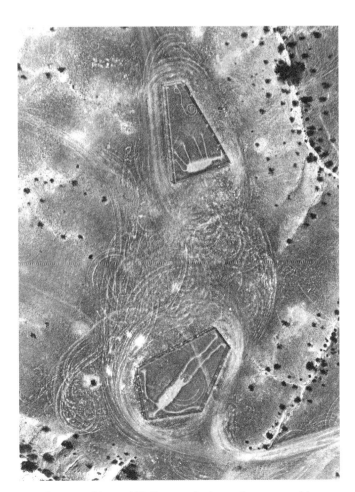

One set of fenced Blythe geoglyphs, anthropomorphic and zoomorphic figures. Extensive damage from off-road vehicles can be seen across the site.

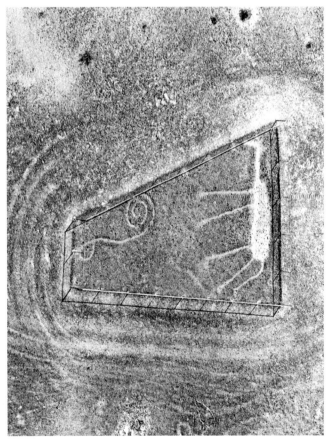

Second zoomorphic figure with a swirl design. Blythe Geoglyph Complex.

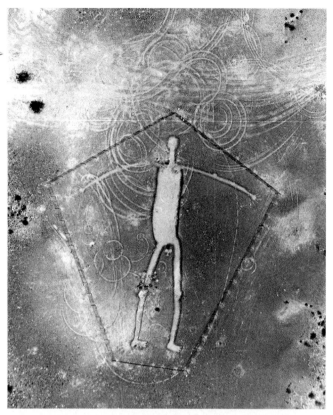

The original position of the right foot was oriented outward, as is the knee. Additionally, the pubic area was originally displayed as a small rock mount; the graphic male genitals are a more recent alteration.

Close-up view of Blythe swirl design. Sometimes thought to be a snake, or possibly a representation of the Colorado River, it is also similar to a Hopi migration symbol. The Hopi claim they left this symbol at sites they occupied along their migration routes.[32]

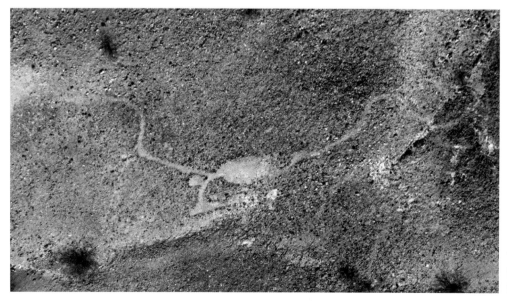

This geoglyph may represent the octopus sent to rid the tribes of the evil giant.

"Double Headed Serpent"

Variously called the "Double Headed Serpent" or the "Flying A," this site is believed to be the result of an activity, such as prolonged use for the same dance pattern, and not a deliberate artistic creation. The geoglyph measures 160 by 114 feet in size.

"Double Headed Serpent." 1982.

"Shaman Geoglyph"

The "Shaman" is located on a terrace overlooking the wide floodplain of the Colorado River, within half a mile of several other geoglyphs. This figure measures 14 by 36 feet in size and is unlike any other anthropomorphic geoglyph in the southwestern United States. It appears to be animated, with the left knee slightly more flexed than the right. Both arms are bent upward at the elbows, the right hand holds what appears to be a snake, while the left hand grips a smaller, unidentifiable object. The gender appears to be male as indicated by the unusually long phallus. There are about six well-defined "sleeping circles" between the geoglyph and Highway 95 and a "mottled" area about 500 yards west of the geoglyph. No ethnographic material has been discovered to help determine the original purpose of this glyph.

Meg Casey at "Shaman Geoglyph" for scale.

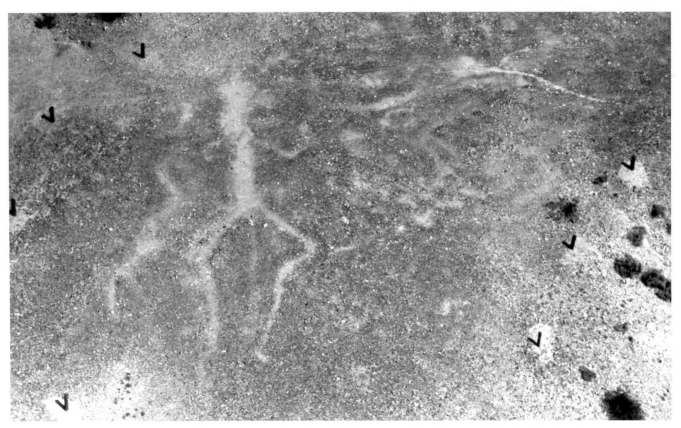

Unusual because of the appearance of motion, this figure may be holding a snake in its right hand.
Mottled areas and sleeping circles are prominent nearby. August 1982.

Anthropomorphic Figure and Dance Circle

Although constructed in a simple stick form, the figure is complete with fingers and toes.

There are at least a dozen larger-than-life geoglyphs representing both humans and animals located immediately north of Blythe. Possibly the most unusual feature in this area is the 30-foot-wide by 560-foot-long area cleared of all desert pavement. The pavement has been raked to the outside edge of the cleared area and left undisturbed.

This small, anthropomorphic stick figure, complete with fingers and toes, rests in the corner of an unusually large area (32 feet by 365 feet) of concentric dance circles. A track-laying construction vehicle turned abruptly when it passed over the head of the figure, apparently not noticing its presence until the last minute.

The tracks of a large construction vehicle are highly visible over the anthropomorphic figure. October 1991.

Anthropomorphic Figure

This site may also commemorate the death of the evil giant who had been harassing the local population. In these photographs, the human figure has his legs dangling over the cliff above the Colorado River. The long zigzag marks to the cliff are said to be the evidence of the final struggle before the octopus dragged the giant into the river.

Long zigzag marks to the cliff edge with an anthropomorphic figure just visible at the edge. August 1982.

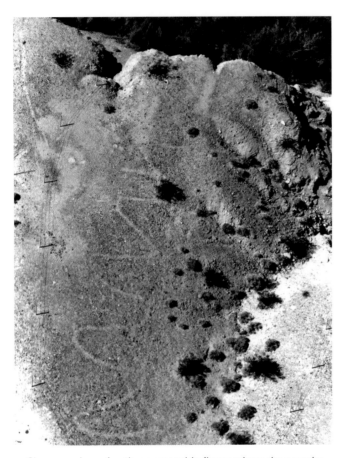

Close-up view of anthropomorphic figure where drag marks and cliff edge meet. August 1982.

"Horseshoe" patterns.

Mule Mountains Site

The area north of the Mule Mountains contains an intriguing mixture of historic and prehistoric creations. Especially controversial are the many "dot" patterns found on one terrace. There are some 240 three-to-four foot cleared circles arranged in two distinct patterns.

One linear pattern is composed of 20 dots, each arranged in two parallel rows of 10 each. They are all nearly equal in size, about 100 feet long by 12 feet wide, and are oriented east to west. The second pattern consists of ten circular or horseshoe shapes. These "footprints" were created using ten three-to-four foot areas cleared of surface gravel to form a semicircular pattern. All are from 20 to 24 feet in diameter and are oriented with the open part of the footprint to the north. However, researchers are not in agreement about the origin of the "dot" patterns. As this was an area of intense military training exercises in 1942, some depressions are likely of military origin.

Far view of Mule Mountain Site with both horseshoe and linear patterns visible. November 1980.

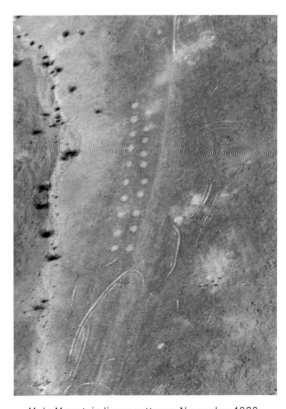

Mule Mountain linear patterns. November 1980.

Ripley Geoglyph Site

Listed on the National Register of Historic Places:
November 20, 1975

This site is located on the bluffs overlooking the east bank of the Colorado River, east of Ripley, California. In 1995, Dr. Ron Dorn dated the construction of the geoglyphs to 1,260 years ago.

The Ripley site includes three anthropomorphic figures, the largest at 118 feet tall; a dance pattern; and a "Maltese Cross." The human figures appear to be missing portions of their bodies: a hand, arm, leg, or head. The Yavapai, who inhabit the mountainous area east of the Colorado River from Parker to almost Yuma, Arizona, used both the Maltese Cross and incomplete human representations in their sand paintings for healing purposes, so these may have come from the same inspirational source.[33]

Articulated anthropomorphic figure with "Maltese Cross."

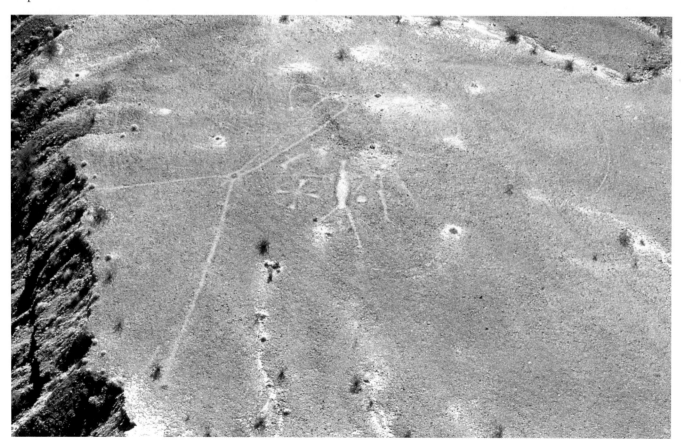

The Ripley Geoglyph Site features an articulated anthropomorphic figure with its right knee flexed. October 1991.

Terrace along the Colorado River ten miles south of Blythe, California.

The two largest anthropomorphic figures in the Ripley complex are situated on a high bluff overlooking the Colorado River south of Blythe.

The largest of the Ripley geoglyphs is 118 feet tall. As with all anthropomorphic geoglyphs along the Colorado River, the legs are oriented toward the river. February 1980.

Topock Maze

Listed in the National Register of Historic Places:
October 5, 1978

The Topock Maze (also called the Indian Maze, Mojave Maze, or Mystic Maze) is situated south of Interstate 40 and the Santa Fe Railroad bridge, west of the Colorado River. It is possibly the most controversial site in regard to origin in our entire study area.[34,35] The Maze, shaped like a "T," covers 18 acres and consists of more than 200 roughly parallel windrows that appear to have been hand-raked into rows of about 8 inches in height, spaced about 5 to 8 feet apart on a pavement-covered terrace.

There are two main stories about this area. Mojave stories claim that this maze was used as a "spiritual cleansing act"[36] in which a person started in the center of the maze and worked his way out to confuse any malignant spirits following him. But skeptics believe that the maze is the result of raking and collecting gravel

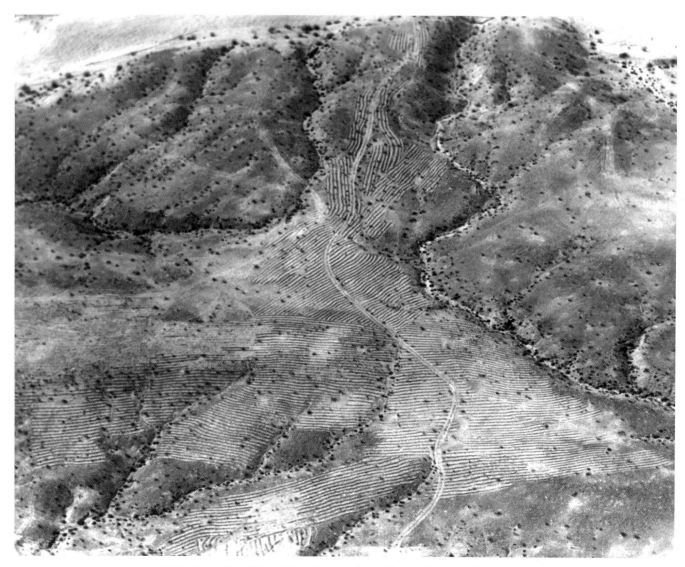

Wide view of the 18 acre Topock Maze site, with a road cutting through it.

to secure building materials for the 1889 construction of the Santa Fe Railroad bridge.[37] Most of the raked windrows north of Interstate 40 have been collected and hauled away to be used elsewhere. Many Mojave elders claim they (the Mojave) did not construct the maze and do not know who did. However, the Mojave confirm that they did occasionally use the maze for ceremonial purposes.

The windrows do not constitute a true maze. There are fifty to sixty rows of gravel raked into parallel lines spaced a small distance apart that converge on similar sets of gravel berms oriented in a slightly differ-ent direction. Occasionally these rows are interrupted by a small gully. The rows resume beyond the gully where the pebbles become more plentiful. Today there are both human and vehicular trails seen throughout the maze. Portions of the maze and similar windrowed gravel collections to the northeast have been removed from the area over the years.

There are many geoglyphs located in this area. Beginning immediately north of the maze are more than a dozen earthen art drawings. Most of these geoglyphs are situated on the California side of the Colorado River.

The windrows do not constitute a true "traditional" maze with an entrance and exit.

February 1990.

Close-up view of gravel berms. Topock Maze.

December 1990.

December 1990.

Anthropomorphic Figure and 6-Point Star

This geoglyph complex is located about one mile northeast of the Topock Maze, on a bluff overlooking the Colorado River. It was severely damaged by vehicles before being fenced in the early 1980s. It incorporates a large anthropomorphic figure, a six-pointed star, and a large dance circle. It is possible this represents the giant and was supposed to be located next to the Topock Maze and was thought to have been destroyed during highway and railroad construction.

Aerial view of anthropomorphic figure with six-pointed star
and fence visible in the upper left of photograph.

The photograph to the left (May 1983) clearly shows the six-pointed star, but does not show a fence.
The protective fence had been added by the time the photograph on the right was taken (February 1990).

Anthropomorphic figure with Meg Casey for scale.

Anthropomorphic Figure

Most human effigies along the Colorado River do not now appear to be very sophisticated. They are usually simple "stick figures": a wide trunk, head, arms, and legs. The hundreds of years of dormancy have had an atrophic affect on the more subtle details of the extremities. Evidence suggests that when first constructed, the figures probably exhibited much more detail: fingers, toes, genitalia, and occasionally hair and head adornments. Even now, many figures appear to be holding something in one hand.

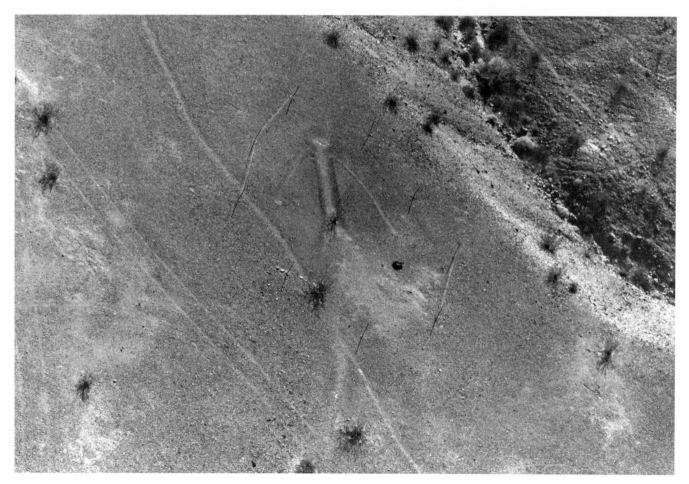

View of geoglyph with trail nearby.

"Moabe Twins" Geoglyph

Many humanoid figures are located near Needles, California, along the Colorado River. The largest of the "Moabe Twins" is thirty feet tall, with a head six feet in diameter. While double figures are quite common along the Colorado River, one is almost always larger than the other, as if they are parent and child. Another unusual pair of humanoid geoglyphs is located across the river and a few miles to the north, near the old Fort Mojave site.

"Moabe Twins" Geoglyph Site.

Aerial view. "Moabe Twins" Geoglyph Site.

Ground view with Meg Casey for scale.

"Fort Mojave Twins"

The most northerly of all the geoglyphs situated along the Colorado River, the "Fort Mojave Twins" are thought to represent the hero twins of the Mojave creation myth. They are unusual not only for their equal size and wide bodies, but for their arrangement of one on top of the other instead of the more typical side by side grouping. Captain Lorenzo Sitgreaves reported seeing these ground drawings on an expedition in 1851.[38]

"Fort Mojave Twins" with Meg Casey for scale. December 1990.

The "Fort Mojave Twins" are unusual for both their equal size and their arrangement of one above the other instead of side by side. August 1982.

Protective fence visible. "Fort Mojave Twins" Site.

"Black Point Site"

The "Black Point" geoglyph complex was a site of intense religious importance to the early Native Americans, and the Mojave still consider the entire area north of Blythe, California, to be sacred ground. Within the elliptical oval of this geoglyph are representations of the Milky Way; the Universe; Mustamho, the Creator God; and Avikwaame, the sacred mountain to the north.

Other, larger geoglyphs north of Blythe are within a mile or two of the Black Point site. They all exhibit the same elliptical shape, and usually have similar north-south lines bisecting the ovals. Within the ovals are often found indistinct geoglyphs. As circular geoglyphs are usually dance circles for ceremonies, it is likely that the figures inside the ovals were the focus of a ceremonial dance, which over time created the distinct elliptical figure.

"Black Point Site" with road graded through site.

The Pilot Knob Complex

The immediate area around this isolated mountain is covered with a very dark mantle of desert pavement, in which are etched at least four humanoid figures, a 156-foot snake-like figure, numerous geometric designs, and a 20-foot-long horse. A trail near the horse geoglyph passes a petroglyph panel of a four-legged animal with a possible rider. The geoglyph and petroglyph are probably of relatively recent age, since the horse was extinct in the Americas until its reintroduction by the Spanish in the 1500s.

In 1990, serious damage was inflicted to the area immediately adjacent the horse geoglyph by vandals. With the help of numerous Quechan volunteers, the disturbed area was painstakingly restored.

Pilot Knob Complex, anthropomorphic geoglyph. June 24, 1979.

Ground view of the anthropomorphic geoglyph being recorded by Jay von Werlhof.

By 2014, the anthropomorphic geoglyph had begun to fade. November 8, 2014. Photograph by Anne Morgan.

Pilot Knob Horse

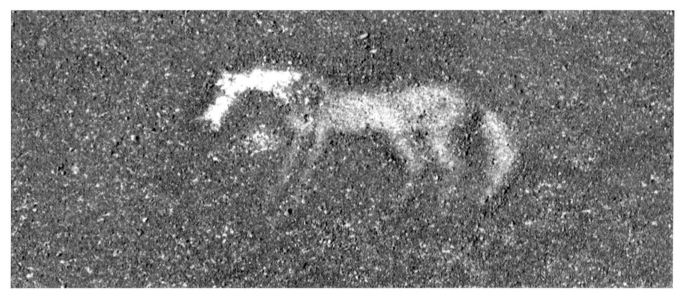

Pilot Knob Complex, Horse Geoglyph.

Ground view. Pilot Knob Complex, Horse Geoglyph.

Aerial view. Pilot Knob Complex, Horse Geoglyph.

Pilot Knob Complex, Horse Geoglyph. April 1983.

Pilot Knob Complex, Horse Geoglyph. May 1990.

Pilot Knob Complex, Horse Geoglyph.

Pilot Knob Snake

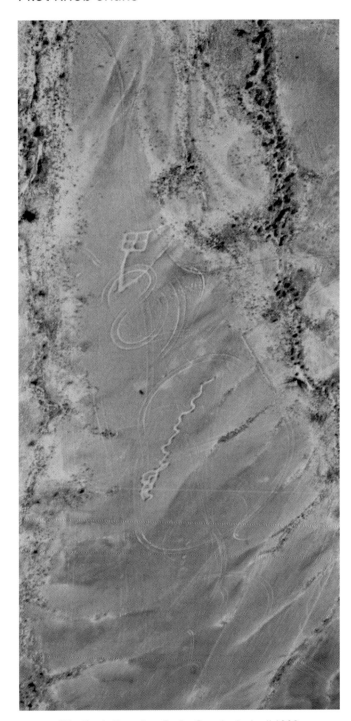

Pilot Knob Complex, Snake Geoglyph. April 1992.

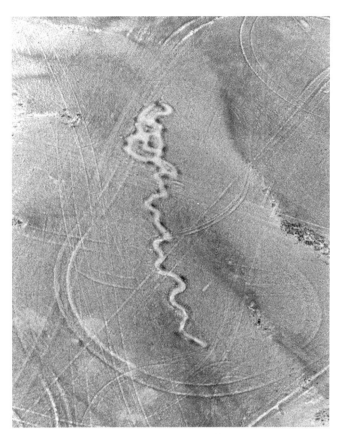

Pilot Knob Complex, Snake Geoglyph with
visible tire track damage. June 25, 1992.

Pilot Knob Complex, Harry Casey recording geometric design.
November 8, 2014. Photograph by Anne Morgan.

"Winterhaven Trail Guardian"

Listed on National Register of Historic Places
May 1, 1987

This 75-foot-tall anthropomorphic geoglyph is often referred to as the "Trail Guardian" or "Winterhaven Stickman." Located on a terrace above the Colorado River floodplain, a well-defined trail runs north-south across the figure at its midpoint. Below the figure are a dozen or so unexplained discolored areas. One possible explanation came about during a lecture, when US Bureau of Land Management Archaeologist Boma Johnson described this figure to his audience. A former military pilot claimed that when practicing aerial gunnery in the area, if he had additional ammunition he would occasionally shoot at the geoglyph. No archaeological surveys have been done to support this claim.

Below the figure is a smaller geoglyph shaped like a Celtic knot. It was constructed using the "tamped-in" method instead of scraping away desert pavement, making it very difficult to see or photograph. No other version of this image has been found in any of the rock art sites in the study area.

Winterhaven "Celtic Knot" with Meg Casey for scale.

The Winterhaven "Celtic Knot" was made using
the "tamped-in" method instead of scraping.

"Winterhaven Trail Guardian" with "Celtic Knot" visible at bottom, a north-south trail
across the center of the figure, and officially unexplained discolored areas.

Anthropomorphic Figure and Trail

Earthen art continues to be discovered in areas that have already been thoroughly surveyed. In this case, a retired couple hiking along an ancient trail north of Winterhaven, California, found this anthropomorphic figure. They reported their find to the appropriate authorities at the Bureau of Land Management in Yuma, Arizona.

Anthropomorphic figure with Meg Casey for scale.

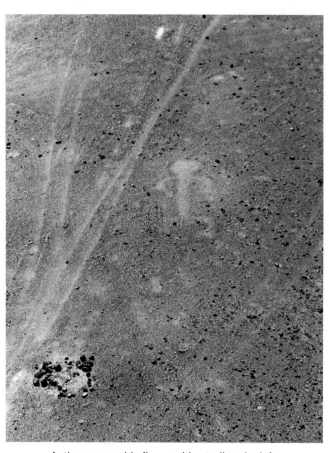

Anthropomorphic figure with a trail to the left.

Stone-Ringed Anthropomorphic Figure

Listed on National Register of Historic Places:
May 1, 1987

North of Yuma, Arizona, on a wide alluvial fan overlooking the Colorado River floodplain, is a larger-than-life-sized human effigy, its head outlined by small stones. No other geoglyph is known to combine the construction techniques of both geoglyphs and rock alignments. The stones around the head may be an aureole denoting that the figure is of a sacred nature.

Anthropomorphic figure with a stone "ring" encircling the head.

Close-up of stone "ring."

"The Fisherman Geoglyph"

This geoglyph was not discovered until July 1984, 25 miles east of the Colorado River and further away from a water source than is normal. Very few ground drawings are this sophisticated. Not only is the figure animated, the site also contains symbols representing the sun, water, fish, and a cloud (or bird). The spear point, 18 by 36 inches in size, was fabricated from more than 150 individual small white quartz stones.

"The Fisherman" may be a recording of the Colorado River creation myth, an important religious story shared by the Colorado River tribes: the Mojave, Chemehuevi, and Quechan. Kustamo (or Mustamho),[39] the Creator God, is said to have made the Colorado River flow "by thrusting a spear into the ground."[40] The Colorado River Indian Tribes Museum in Parker, Arizona, contains a display that states: "Mustamho stirred and compressed darkness to form sky and earth. Male sky lay over female earth and the offspring was… Matavilla…creator of man."[41]

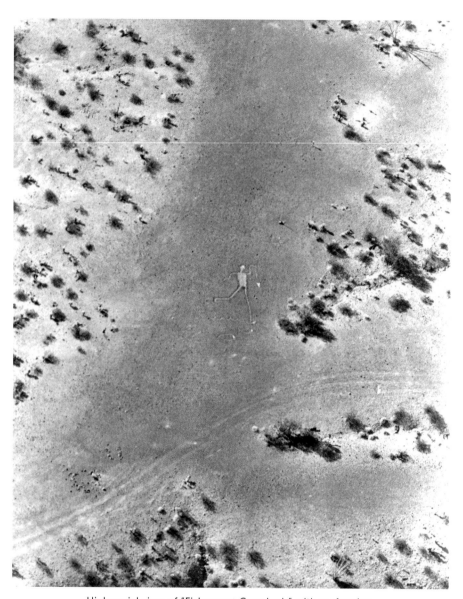

High aerial view of "Fisherman Geoglyph" with no fencing.

Ground view of "Fisherman Geoglyph" with fencing.

Close-up of quartz spear point.

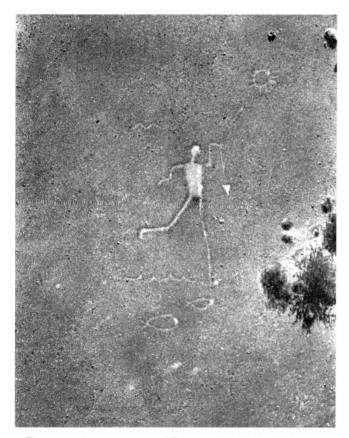

The unusual sun, waves, and fish are all visible in this image.

The Bureau of Land Management
fenced this geoglyph for its protection.

Mojave River Channel Site

Located along the Mojave River channel, east of Barstow, California, this site includes a large anthropomorphic figure, a quadruped (possibly a bighorn sheep), an apparent bear claw, a well-defined spiral shape, and a barbell-shaped glyph.

Some of these symbols were regularly used by groups of Hopi to denote clan affiliations.[42] These drawings, if indeed they are the works of Native Americans, could indicate that the usually dry Mojave River channel was an important migration route for certain Native American groups traveling from the Colorado River to the Pacific coast.

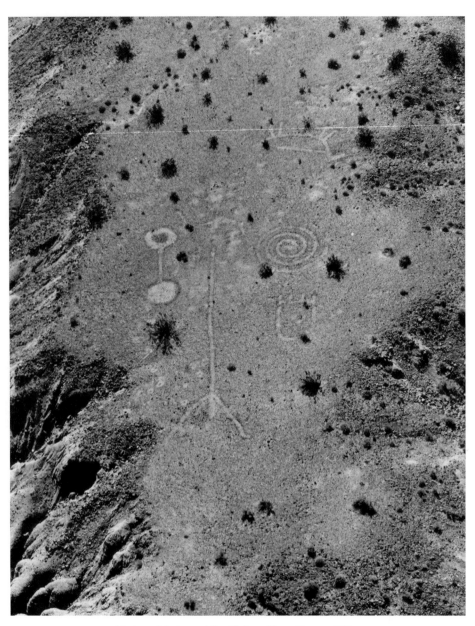

High aerial view of the Mojave River Channel Site.

Ground view with people for scale.

This figure is exactly like that of the Hopi Bear Claw clan.

Close-up of spiral and "bear claw" portion of site. The spiral is similar to petroglyphs made by the Hopi to indicate a migration.

Close-up of zoomorphic figure, similar to bighorn sheep petroglyphs in Arizona.

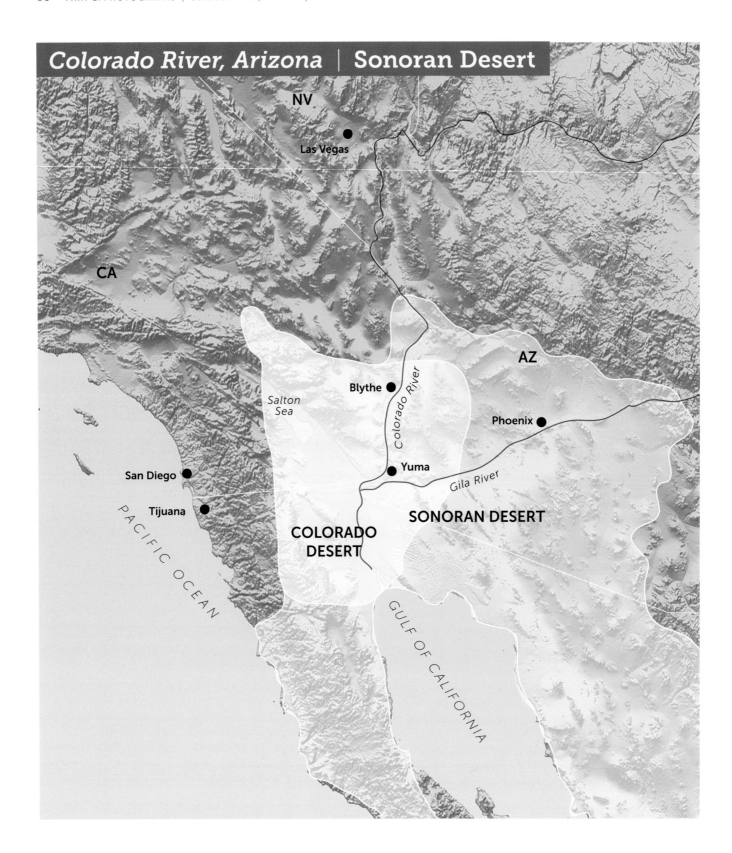

Colorado River, Arizona | Sonoran Desert

NV

Las Vegas

CA

AZ

Salton Sea

Blythe

Colorado River

Phoenix

San Diego

Yuma

Gila River

Tijuana

PACIFIC OCEAN

SONORAN DESERT

COLORADO DESERT

GULF OF CALIFORNIA

Colorado River, Arizona
Sonoran Desert

"Parker Snake Geoglyph"

One of the more sophisticated geoglyph designs is this 150-foot-long rattlesnake. Snake symbols are not usually depicted in detail but this figure has defined coils at the tail and for a time included a forked tongue. The head features two large stone eyes that some Mojave claim are so powerful that they glow in the dark.

An enigma to researchers because of its fine details and location further than usual from the Colorado River, it is possible this geoglyph has been altered over the centuries.

A forked tongue can be seen faintly
in this image. February 1990.

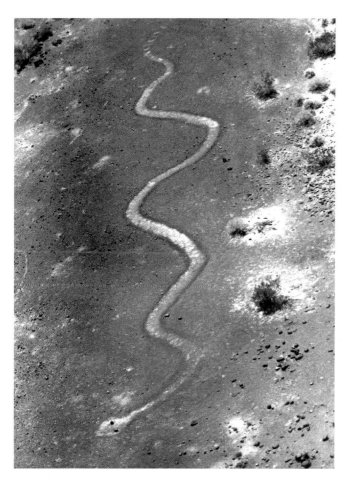

A forked tongue can be faintly seen in this image. The quartz
eyes are visible in the head and coils are visible at the tail.

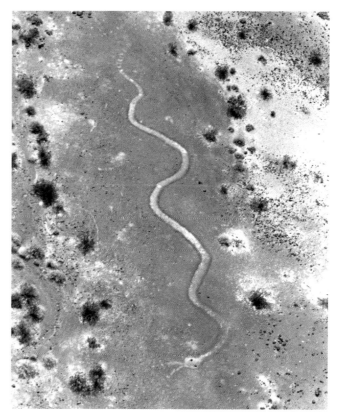

A forked tongue is clearly seen when
this picture was taken (date unknown).

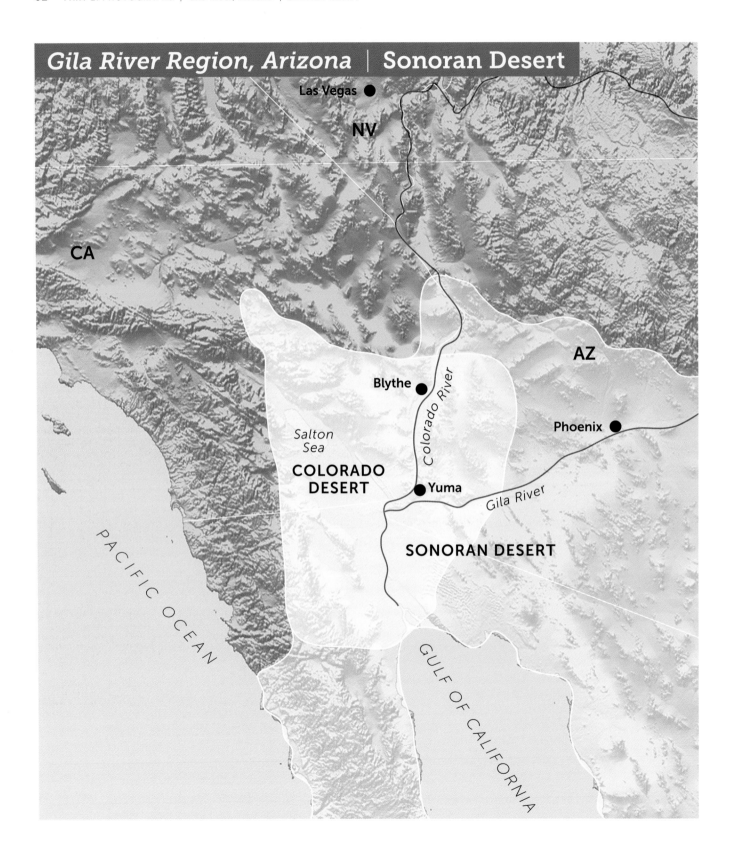

Gila River Region, Arizona | Sonoran Desert

Gila River Region, Arizona
Sonoran Desert

This area, southwest of Painted Rock State Park in southwestern Arizona, is the site of many forms of rock art. On the plateau overlooking the wide floodplain of the Gila River are many rock alignments and "avenidas." On the flat rock faces below the cliff may be found countless petroglyphs. The traditional Native American inhabitants of the Gila River were the Yuma (Quechan), Cocopah, Papago, Pima, and Maricopa peoples. These groups, and their ancestors, are responsible for the prolific rock art in the area.

"Bicycle Geoglyph"

It has been suggested that this intricate design may have been created by a complicated dance pattern.

The unusually complex spiral design is similar to two Hopi symbols representing migration and Mother Earth. The Hopi migration symbol not only indicated the number of times the site was visited, but the direction of travel, intermediate stops, and the approximate length of the stay. Assuming the above geoglyph is a Hopi migration symbol, the site was visited at least six times (indicated by the number of spirals).[43] The Mother Earth or "emergence symbol" of the Hopi, Pima, and many other tribes symbolizes birth or rebirth from one world to the next.

"Bicycle Geoglyph." November 1990.

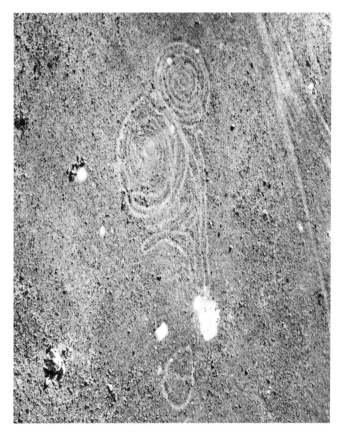

"Bicycle Geoglyph."

"Sacaton Woman Geoglyph"

These figures are the most easterly of all known geoglyphs in our study area. The largest figure is 105 feet in height; the second is 14 feet tall. Cairns mark the head, foot, and hand areas of both figures. The larger humanoid figure has two additional piles of stones along its lengthy body.

Pima (Papago) tribe mythology suggests that this ground drawing was created by (or because of) the evil giant Haak Vaak. Two myths exist about this geoglyph.[44] The first says that Haak Vaak was a cannibal who devoured children and that, when Elder Brother killed Haak Vaak, the ground drawing was constructed to commemorate the event. The second myth states that Haak Vaak slept at this site one night, leaving the depressed outline of the giant.[45]

High aerial view. "Sacaton Woman Geoglyph."

Close-up of smaller figure. "Sacaton Woman Geoglyph."

Several geoglyphs have recently been discovered west of Phoenix, Arizona. The topography in this area is very sandy, flat desert with occasional dark rocky hills protruding from the desert floor. The site is about eight miles northwest of the point where the Gila River makes a 90-degree turn and heads south toward Gila Bend.

Geoglyph similar to "JJ Carr" in appearance.

Geoglyph, possibly a large anthropomorphic figure.

Fish:

Ground view, with person for scale. "Fish Geoglyph."

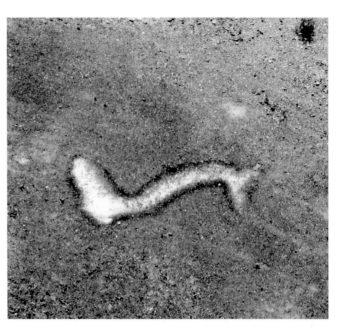

"Fish Geoglyph." July 1982.

Quail:

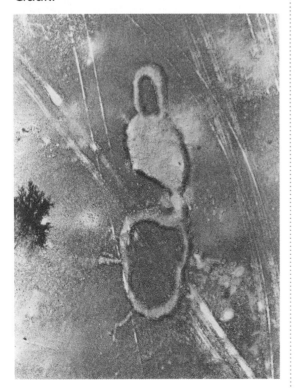

"Quail Geoglyph."

Reptile:

This geoglyph may represent a reptile.
Notice the well-traveled trail system to the right of the geoglyph.
Trails are often in close proximity to ground drawings.

"JJ Carr Intaglio":

This figure, known as the "J.J. Carr Intaglio," is located along the Gila River east of Yuma, Arizona. Very little is known about this particular ground drawing. While it is located in an area where other geoglyphs are present, the "unfaded" condition, wide lines, and unusual shape of the drawing make its authenticity questionable. Unfortunately, this 70-by-230 foot drawing may have been lost due to recent expansion of a nearby sand and gravel operation.

"J.J. Carr Intaglio." September 1981.

Avenidas

"Avenidas" are cleared paths, three or four feet wide and about 50 to 100 feet long. They begin suddenly for no apparent reason and end at the edge of a cliff. The "avenida" phenomenon is widespread along the Gila River channel west of Painted Rock Dam in Arizona. They are often found in the vicinity of alignments, trails, and areas where Native Americans held sporting events.

Example of avenida at cliff edge.

This site was probably an important ceremonial area. Notice the numerous cairns, habitation areas, avenidas, and undulating lines, which were probably the result of prolonged dancing.

Rock Alignments
Alignment with double figures

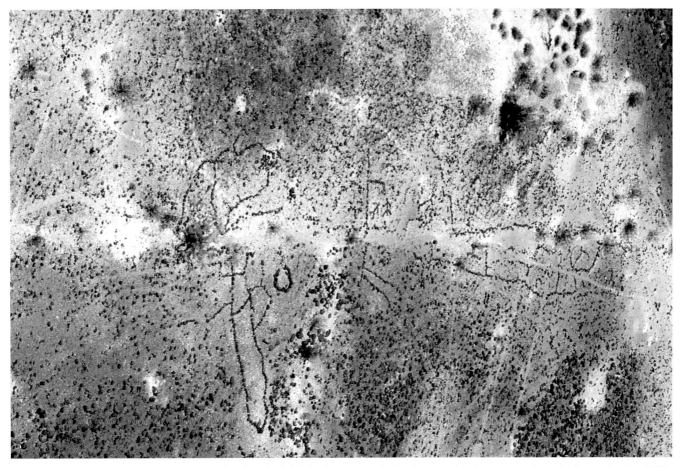

The anthropomorphic "Double Figures" are just barely visible in the center of this photograph, above the main rock alignment. May 1988.

Jay von Werlhof recording anthropomorphic figures in the alignment. The small figures were not seen in the original aerial reconnaissance, but only after enlargements were viewed with a magnifying glass. These "darkroom discoveries" are often just as exciting as the "in situ" discoveries.

Compartmentalized rock alignment

Compartmentalized rock alignment. January 1991.

The compartmentalized alignment is contained within a wide symmetrical half circle that opens toward the cliff. A row of rocks leads from the edge of the cliff to the center of the alignment.

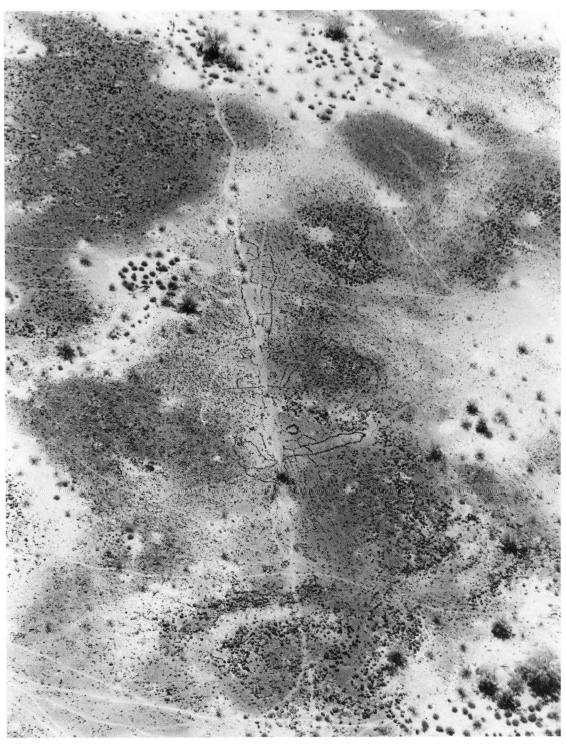

In the Gila Bend area, there appears to be a preponderance of rock alignments.
Conversely, along the Colorado River the geoglyph is the dominant form of earthen art.

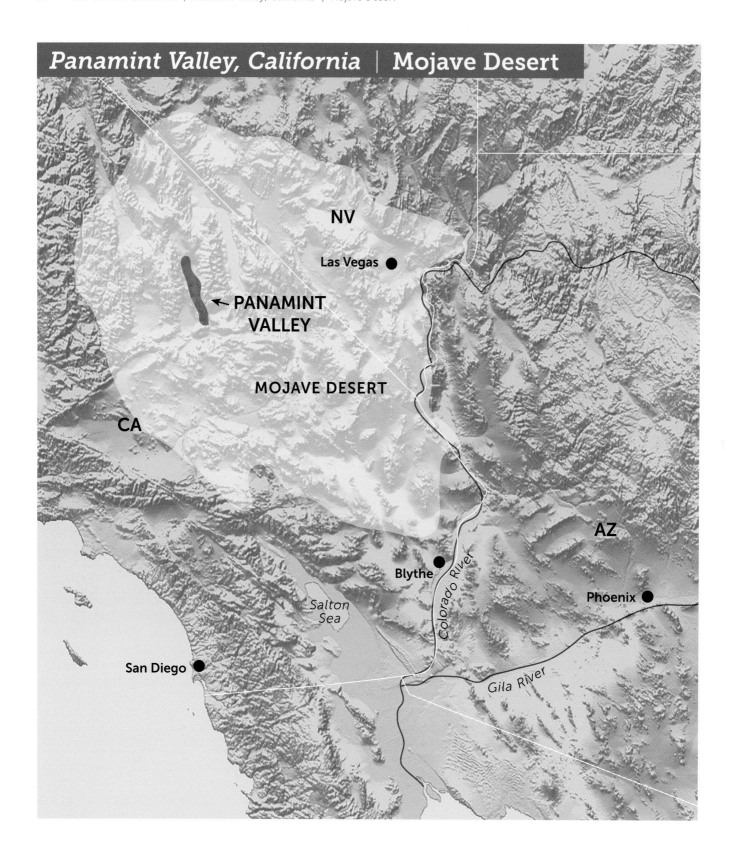

Panamint Valley, California | Mojave Desert

NV

Las Vegas ●

← PANAMINT VALLEY

MOJAVE DESERT

CA

AZ

Blythe ●

Colorado River

Salton Sea

Phoenix ●

San Diego ●

Gila River

Panamint Valley, California
Mojave Desert

The Panamint Valley, located in the extreme north-west portion of the Mojave Desert, west of Death Valley, contains an unusually large quantity of relatively sophisticated rock alignments. There are probably more complex rock patterns in the Panamint Valley than in all the rest of our study area combined. Although numerically the Panamint Valley contains about thirty of the 120 known alignments in our study area, more than half of these are unusually complex designs. These alignments are also possibly the oldest in our study area, as they are heavily varnished on their exposed sides and deeply embedded in the surrounding desert pavement.

No two alignments in the Panamint Valley are alike. Some are carefully made, long, undulating lines of rocks placed so closely together that they touch one another. Although these have been clearly constructed with great care, modern ethnographers are unable to explain what they represent or why they were made.

Earthen art is usually found in remote locations, separated by miles between images. The Panamint Valley alignments, however, consist of more than thirty alignments found in a relatively narrow band above the old shoreline of an extinct Pleistocene lake.

Barstow Rock Alignment

Unlike most of the older rock alignments found in the Mojave Desert, this alignment is not situated along the shoreline of an extinct Pleistocene lake. The rocks of this alignment are heavily varnished and deeply embedded in the surrounding desert pavement. Additionally, the undersides of the stones display a bright orange coating of ground patina, which indicates that this alignment is older than most found in the southern Mojave Desert.

Barstow Rock Alignment. April 1992.

Panamint Valley Rock Alignments

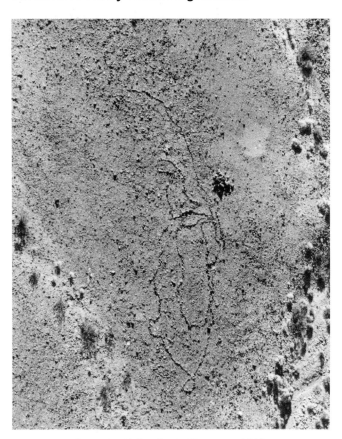

Panamint Valley Rock Alignment. 1982.

Panamint Valley Rock Alignment.

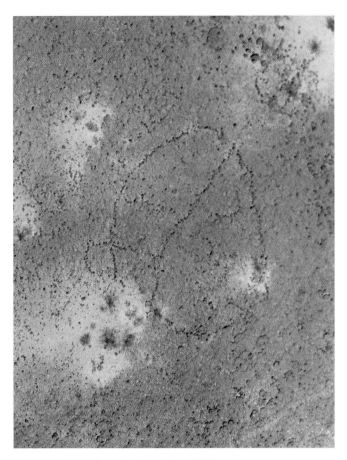

Panamint Valley Rock Alignment.

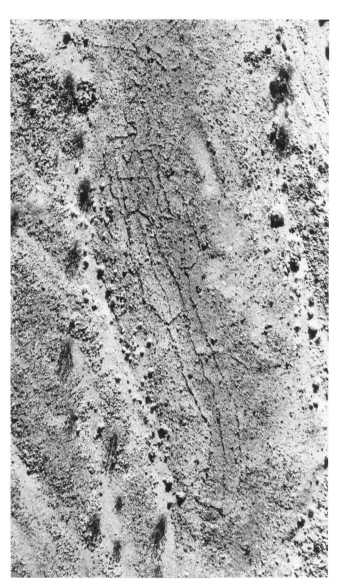

Panamint Valley Rock Alignment.

Close-up of rock alignment with Meg Casey for scale.
Panamint Valley Rock Alignment.

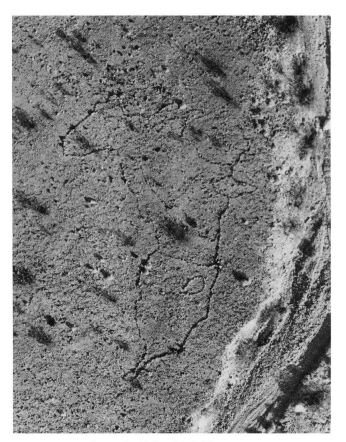

Panamint Valley Rock Alignment.

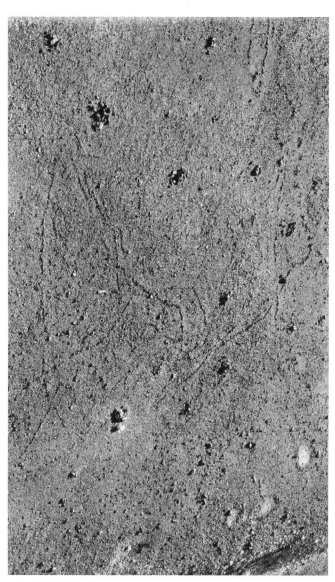

Panamint Valley Rock Alignment.

Panamint Valley Rock Alignment with Meg Casey for scale.

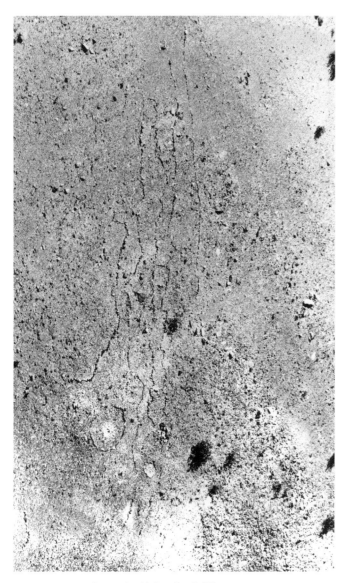

Panamint Valley Rock Alignment.

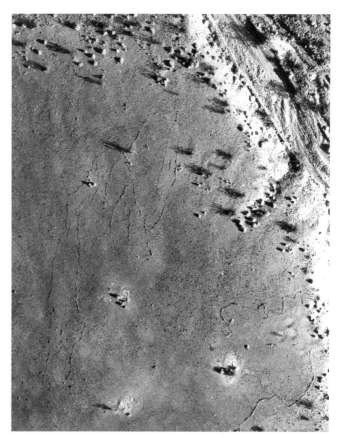

Panamint Valley Rock Alignment.

Panamint Valley Rock Alignment with trail.

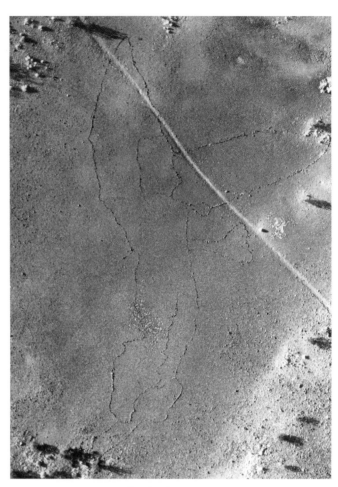

Panamint Valley Rock Alignment.

Panamint Valley Rock Alignment with trail.

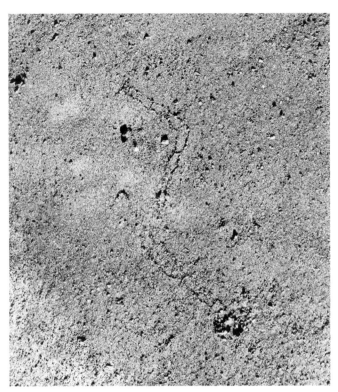

Panamint Valley Rock Alignment.

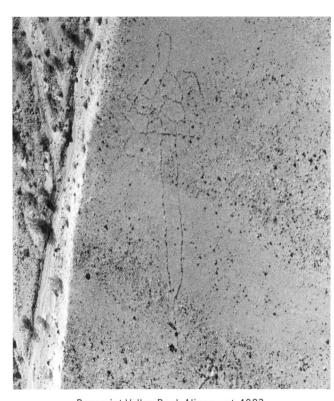

Panamint Valley Rock Alignment. 1982.

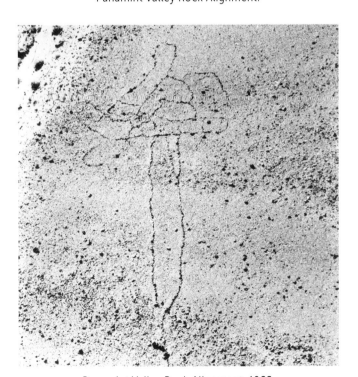

Panamint Valley Rock Alignment. 1982.

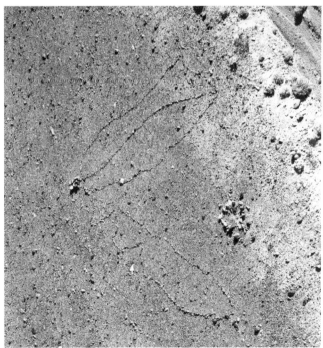

Panamint Valley Rock Alignment. 1983.

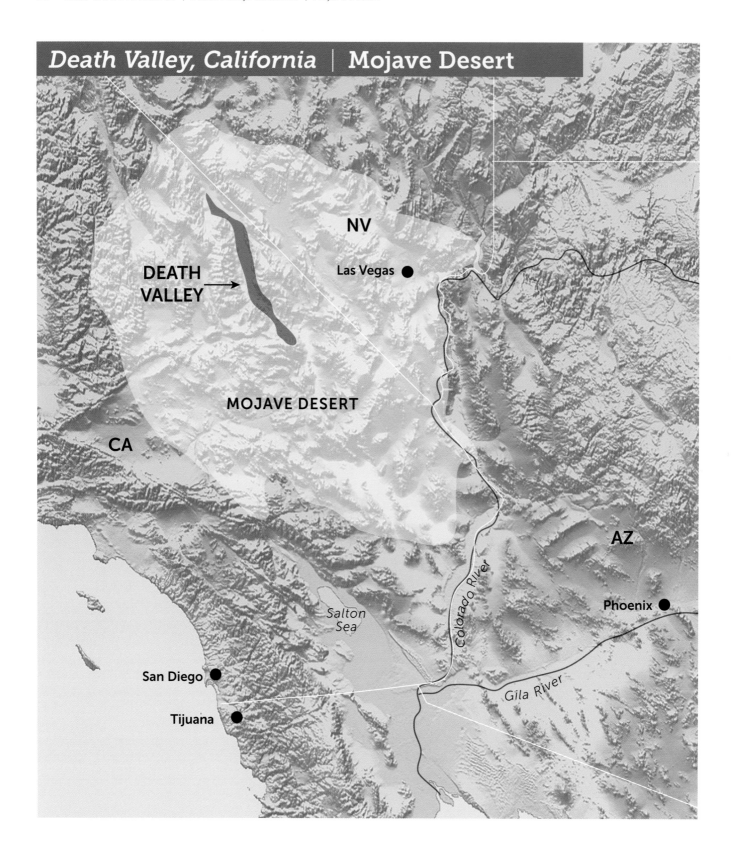

Death Valley, California | **Mojave Desert**

DEATH VALLEY →

NV

Las Vegas ●

MOJAVE DESERT

CA

AZ

Colorado River

Phoenix ●

Salton Sea

San Diego ●

Gila River

Tijuana ●

Death Valley, California
Mojave Desert

Death Valley is the location of an amazing quantity of earthen art. This may seem incongruous considering the inhospitable nature of the area today. However, as recently as 10,000 years ago, the entire valley was covered by the freshwater Lake Manly.

Geoglyphs are relatively rare in the Mojave Desert, especially in comparison to the number of rock alignments.

Rock alignments in Death Valley are located above the ancient shoreline of Lake Manly. The bottom of the lake bed is 282 feet below sea level, the lowest point in the United States.

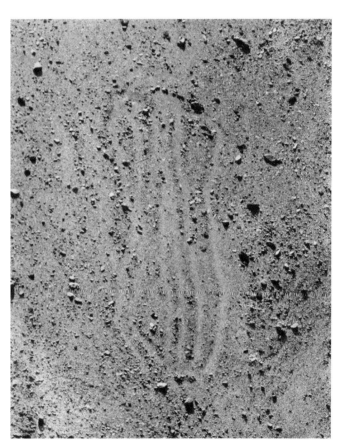

There are no geoglyphs similar to this 54 x20 foot figure.

Death Valley Rock Alignment.

Death Valley Rock Alignment.

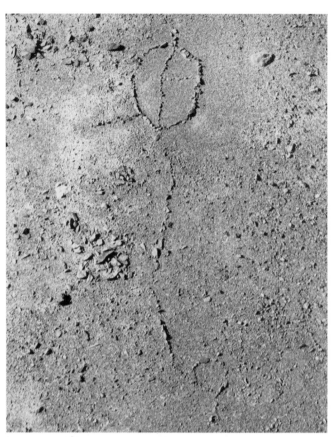

Death Valley Rock Alignment.

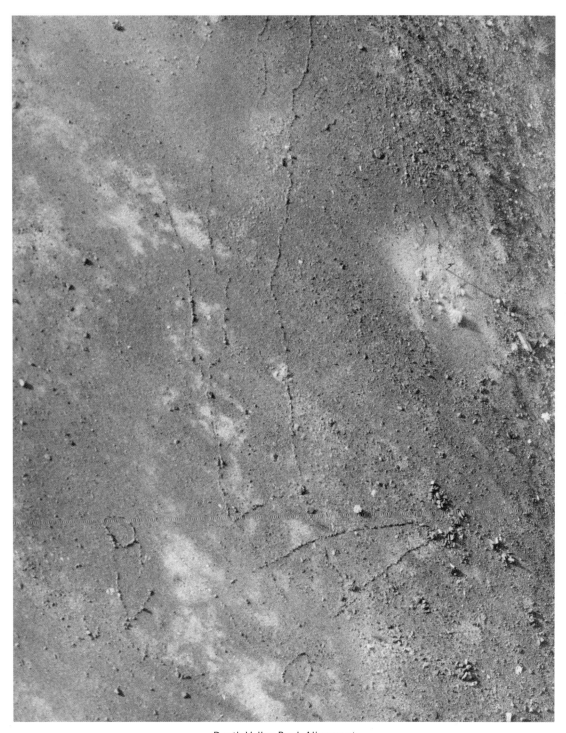

Death Valley Rock Alignment.

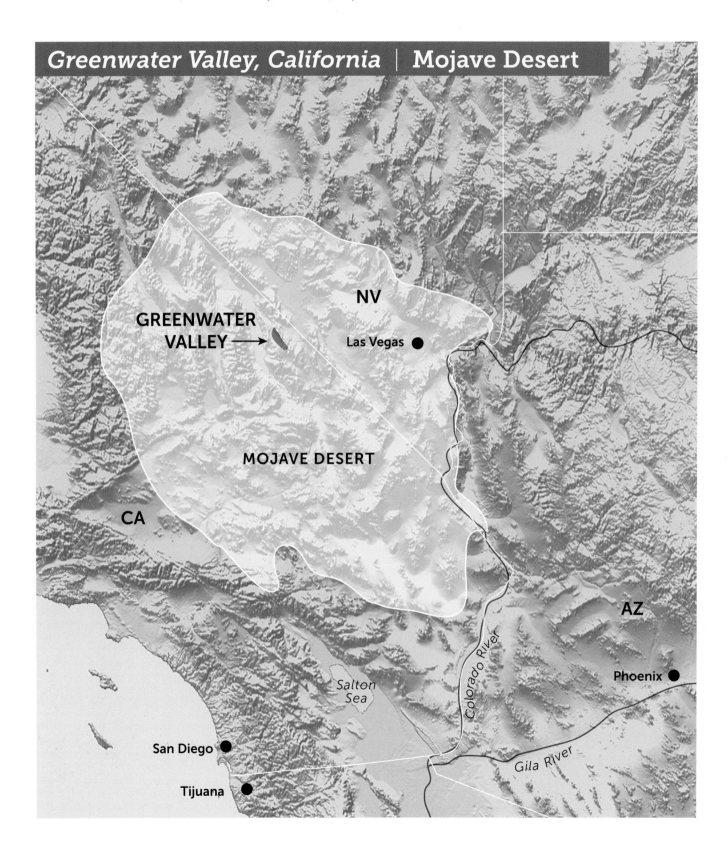

Greenwater Valley, California | Mojave Desert

GREENWATER VALLEY →

NV

Las Vegas ●

MOJAVE DESERT

CA

AZ

Salton Sea

Colorado River

Phoenix ●

San Diego ●

Gila River

Tijuana ●

Greenwater Valley, California
Mojave Desert

Greenwater Valley is located just east of Death Valley and stretches similarly in a north-south direction. There are two rock alignments about a quarter of a mile apart in the southern portion of Greenwater Valley. However, only the northernmost appears to be archaic. Based on the desert varnish, the other site is most likely the result of more modern visitors to the valley.

Greenwater Valley Rock Alignment.

Greenwater Valley Rock Alignment.

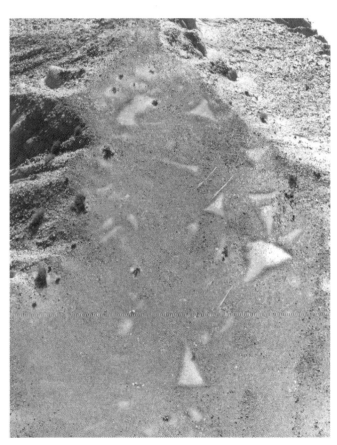

Triangular areas east of Barstow, California.

SIMILARITIES IN APPEARANCE

One approach to the analysis of unknowns is to amass an inventory of images that contain similarities. This comparison of features is an aid in categorizing a bewildering quantity of diverse earthen art figures.

Rock alignments, for example, rarely represent anything familiar to researchers. Notable exceptions are the six or more widely scattered anthropomorphic figures. All these stone outlines of the human form are either life-sized or smaller, while similar anthropomorphic geoglyphs are usually much larger.

Rarely do alignments represent anything recognizable to the modern observer.
However, this alignment along the Gila River contains a life-sized pair of humanoid figures within its confines.
A major east-to-west trail system passes directly through the alignment. December 1990.

This animated "running man" figure is located next to the alignment that archaeologist Malcolm Rogers recorded as SDM-C-70 in eastern Imperial County, California. Since the human figure was not mentioned in Rogers' site records, it is suspected of being a recent addition.

The figure encircled by the rocks is located east of Parker, Arizona. It was not discovered until early in 1980. This again raises the question of its authenticity.

Arrows are predominantly found in geoglyphs, although there are a few made of stones. There are at least a dozen arrow glyphs scattered throughout our study area. Some are near the Colorado and Gila Rivers, while an equal number are located in Death Valley.

Palo Verde Arrow, Imperial Valley. Meg Casey for scale.

Quartzite Arrow Site. Colorado River area, California.

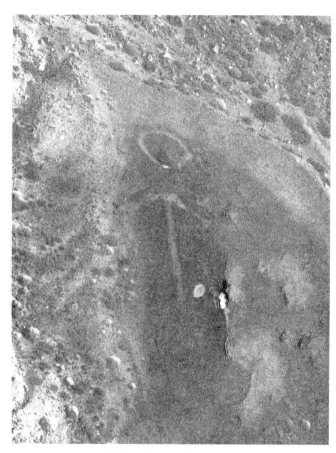

Mojave Desert, California.

Quartzite Arrow Site.
Colorado River area, California.

There are several concentric circle geoglyphs scattered throughout the southern portion of our study area. However, none of them seems to be very closely related in either location or appearance.

Concentric circles, Imperial Valley. Meg Casey for scale.

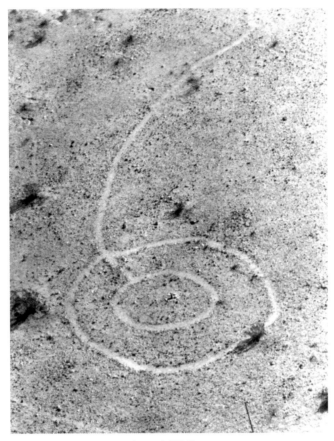

Imperial Valley.

Colorado River area, California.

The most common ground drawings are the nearly fifty anthropomorphic figures along the Colorado River. Some appear as pairs, with one of the figures generally larger than the other. Usually they are "stick" figures, sometimes the body will have been enlarged. Rarely are any details such as fingers or toes visible today.

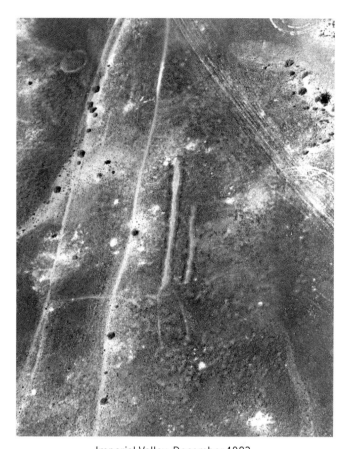
Imperial Valley. December 1982.

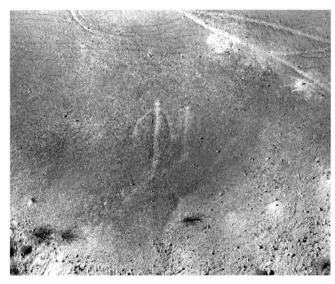
Colorado River area, California.

Colorado River area, California. July 1985.

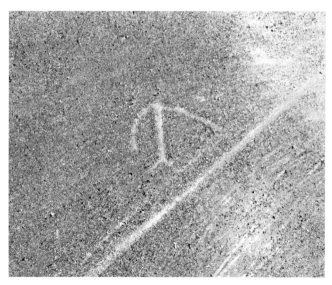
Colorado River area, California.

THE GEOGLYPH AUTHENTICITY PROBLEM

The primary question to consider when studying earthen art is: When was it built? Older historic manifestations, for example, are often confused with the works of prehistoric Native Americans. Some geoglyphs appear to be fading much faster than others. These, obviously, are problematic in origin. There are many geoglyphs that are classified as legitimate "ancient" earthen art simply because it is "safer" to do so. The figure, if treated as authentic, is at least assured some degree of physical protection and can be subjected to intense scrutiny in the future.

Compounding this authenticity problem is the fact that human travel has caused more desert disfigurement in the last 100 years than ever before. Desert training maneuvers during World War II created many confusing ground disturbances that are still visible today.[46] The presence of old military campsites, tank tracks, foxholes, and other unexplained complex surface designs interspersed with ancient Native American trails and habitation sites create a very serious interpretative problem.

The likelihood of discovering a "counterfeit" geoglyph such as those below is always possible.

This anthropomorphic figure is unlikely to be mistaken for a prehistoric gcoglyph. Imperial Valley.

This "happy face" figure is unlikely to be mistaken for a prehistoric qeoqlyph. Imperial Valley. August 1986.

"Joe T." is an example of a modern work not likely to be mistaken for a prehistoric geoglyph. Imperial Valley.

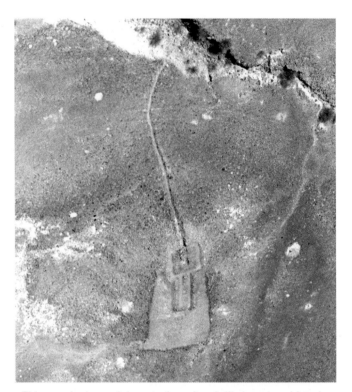

This geoglyph, reminiscent of a guitar, is likely not prehistoric. Unlike the "happy face" image however, it is not certain. Imperial Valley.

This photograph (right) illustrates a confusing authenticity problem. More than sixty-five years ago small patches of desert pavement were hand-raked into large piles and removed from this area to be used elsewhere. The scars left by this gravel-collecting operation look somewhat similar to geoglyphs.[47]

Scars from gravel-removing operation. Imperial Valley.

The precision with which this alignment (below) was constructed makes its authenticity questionable. Most alignments in the southwestern United States were not built with equal-sized stones spaced as precisely as in this alignment. Additionally, there are four larger flat stones strategically placed along the perimeter of the circle at exactly 90 degrees. Upon these flat stones were placed small quartz rocks and shells. It is unlikely for these small stones and shells to have remained there for any lengthy period. However, the most distinctive feature of this unusual alignment is one small flat cobble upon which is painted the Oriental yin-yang symbol.

Close-up of quartz stones placed on one of the large, flat stones within alignment. Note the yin-yang symbol painted on one stone. Greenwater Valley, Mojave Desert.

Most prehistoric alignments in the southwestern United States were not built as precisely as this alignment. Greenwater Valley, Mojave Desert.

BIOGRAPHY | HARRY CASEY

Harry Casey with telescoping pole for cameras. May 1991.

I am the eldest of three sons born into a farming family east of Brawley, California. My brothers chose professional careers while I elected to stay on the farm. My interests in flying, photography, and desert archaeology led me to take classes from Jay von Werlhof at Imperial Valley College in El Centro, California. During these classes, I met my (future) wife, Margaret and made a lifelong friend in Jay. For the last thirty-five years, I have been flying over the lower reaches of the Colorado and Gila Rivers and both the Colorado and Mojave Deserts searching for evidence of past cultures.

I hope that my photographic quest has contributed to a better understanding about the quantity and sophistication of a fading artistic expression, unique to the extreme southwestern United States.

To perpetuate earthen art research, I am donating my photographic collection and research materials to the Imperial Valley Desert Museum in Ocotillo, California. This extensive collection includes thousands of black-and-white photographic enlargements of geoglyphs and rock alignments, as well as negatives and color slides. Additionally, my comprehensive collection of books, articles, and correspondence regarding earthen art research will be given to the museum for future researchers. Hopefully, this material will form the nucleus of a local earthen art research center at the museum. I am confident that the Imperial Valley Desert Museum will become an important center for future earthen art research.

BIOGRAPHY | ANNE MORGAN

Anne Morgan, Head Archivist and Curator at the
Imperial Valley Desert Museum, Ocotillo, California. 2017.

Born and raised in New Orleans, Louisiana, Anne grew up with two major passions: history and animals. The love of history she got from her parents, the love of animals from her many rescue dogs and ferrets. She attended Lake Forest College in Lake Forest, Illinois and earned a degree in History, with a minor in Comparative Religion. Encouraged by her parents and mentor, Professor Ron Miller, she then went on to Simmons College in Boston, Massachusetts, for a Masters in Library and Information Science, focusing on archives. A chance meeting with a Simmons alum at a Society of American Archivists conference led her to take a three-month internship at a new museum in a place she'd never heard of: Imperial Valley. Anne fell in love with the desert and went from being an intern to the Head Archivist/Curator at the Imperial Valley Desert Museum, in Ocotillo, California. While working at the museum in 2012 Anne met Harry and Meg Casey and what began as a simple archival project of Harry's nearly 10,000 aerial images became a friendship and partnership as she helped edit Harry's original manuscript, *Earthen Art of the Extreme Southwest*, into the book you are holding today. In addition to her work as an archivist and curator, Anne's passions are hiking the desert and supporting local animal shelters—working to bring awareness of animal cruelty issues to the public and to legalize ferrets in the state of California.

CONTRIBUTORS TO EARTHEN ART STUDIES

Jay von Werlhof in the field.
December 1990.

Jay von Werlhof: A professor of history, anthropology, and archaeology at Imperial Valley College in El Centro, California for 19 years, von Werlhof influenced hundreds of college students and archaeology enthusiasts—this author included. An early director of the Imperial Valley College-Barker Museum, he conducted field research in remote areas throughout the Mojave and Colorado Deserts, and recorded over 10,000 previously undocumented archaeological sites in Imperial County.

Boma Johnson: Johnson was an archaeologist with the Bureau of Land Management in Yuma, Arizona, for 25 years, and active in earthen art research since 1976. He researched rock art throughout the Southwest and discovered countless ethnographic ties between geoglyphs and Native Indian mythology.

Dr. Ron Dorn: Professor of Geography and Co-Coordinator of the Arizona Geographic Alliance at Arizona State University since 1988, Dorn developed a radiocarbon dating technique that allows rock art, including geoglyphs, to be dated with accuracy.

Dr. Persis B. Clarkson: A Professor of Anthropology at the University of Winnipeg in Canada, Dr. Clarkson is also an archaeologist and geoglyph expert. She has worked and published with Dr. Ron Dorn on radiocarbon dating rock varnish.

Dr. E.L. Davis: "Davey" devoted a great deal of time and energy to archaeological research in the Mojave Desert. She was especially interested in the Panamint Valley alignments, which she called "geoscript" because she believed they might be a form of hieroglyphics that conceivably could be decoded.

Dan McCarthy: University of California at Riverside archaeologist and coordinator for the California Archaeology Inventory, McCarthy has continued much of Dr. Davis' study of early man in the Mojave Desert.

Piper J-3 "Cub": The author's beloved 1946 Piper J-3 "Cub" was used for aerial reconnaissance for more than thirty years (almost 800 flying hours). This antique, fabric-covered aircraft had no electrical system and the engine had to be started by turning the propeller by hand. Although old and slow, the aircraft proved to be a dependable, maneuverable machine that afforded excellent visibility, especially when the door and window were opened. It was possible to take photographs through a hole cut in the floor of the cabin.

This aircraft, more than any other single piece of equipment, made this earthen art recording attempt a success.

Piper J-3 "Cub." February 1980.

ENDNOTES

[1] John Clegg, Senior Lecturer at the Department of Anthropology, University of Sydney, was instrumental in helping the author obtain photocopies of journal articles from the Australian Institute of Aboriginal Studies, located in Canberra, Australia. This information on Australian "stone arrangements" was of great help to the author.

[2] McCarthey, Frederick D., 1940. "Aboriginal Stone Arrangements in Australia." *Australian Museum Magazine.* 7(5):184-189.

[3] VandenDolder, Evelyn M., 1992. "Rock Varnish and Desert Pavement Provide Geological and Archaeological Records." *Arizona Geology.* 22(1):1-9.

[4] Dorn, Ronald I., 1991. "Rock Varnish." *American Scientist.* 79(6):542-553.

[5] Exceptions are the unusually large pictographs found in the midriff area of Baja California, Mexico.

[6] Dorn, Ronald I., Persis B. Clarkson, Margaret F. Nobbs, Lawrence L. Loendorf, and D.S. Whitley, 1992. "New Approach to the Radiocarbon Dating of Rock Varnish with Examples from Drylands." *Annals of the Association of American Geographers.* 82(1):136-151.

[7] Ron Dorn, personal communication, Dec. 1990. Each accelerator radiocarbon date costs $500.

[8] Dorn. "Rock Varnish."

[9] Dorn. "Rock Varnish." p. 545.

[10] Pablo F. Cerda, earthen art researcher, Santiago, Chile, in a letter to Harry Casey 14 Sept. 1987.

[11] Johnson, Boma, 1985. *Earth Figures of the Lower Colorado and Gila River Deserts: A Functional Analysis.* Arizona Archaeological Society, Yuma. pp. 6-9.

[12] Davis, Emma Lou and Clark W. Brott, 1982. "Shamanic Dreams and Drying Lakes." Individual Abstract at the Society for California Archaeology. San Diego, California, March 24, 1982.

[13] Hudson, Travis, Georgia Lee, and Ken Hedges, 1979. "Solstice Observers and Observations in Native California." *Journal of California and Great Basin Anthropology.* 1(1):39.

[14] Haenszel, Arda M., 1981. "Series of Ground Figures in Mohave Valley." *Archaeological Survey Association Journal.* 5(1):20-25.

[15] "Regional Natural History: The Sonoran Desert Region and Its Subdivisions." *Arizona-Sonoran Desert Museum.* Arizona-Sonoran Desert Museum. https://www.desert-museum.org/desert/sonora.php. Accessed 6 September 2017.

[16] Waters, Michael R., 1983. "Late Holocene Lacustrine Chronology and Archaeology of Ancient Lake Cahuilla, California." *Quarternary Research.* 19(3):373-387.

[17] Salton Sea Authority, 1997. "The Salton Sea: A Brief Description of Its Condition and Potential Remediation Projects." The Salton Sea Authority. 3 October 1997 *SDSU Center for Inland Waters Salton Basin-Colorado Delta.* http://www.sci.sdsu.edu/salton/Salton%20Sea%20Description.html. Accessed 7 September 2017.

[18] National Oceanic and Atmospheric Administration. "Perspectives Global Warming Home: Mid-Holocene Warm Period." https://www.ncdc.noaa.gov/global-warming/mid-holocene-warm-period. Accessed 3 November 2017.

[19]Von Werlhof, Jay, Casey Nopah, and Welton Johnson, 1982. "Two Worlds of Archaeology: A Case Study." Presented to the Society for California Archaeology, Sacramento, California: April 2, 1982.

[20]Heizer, Robert F., 1953. "Additional Surface Intaglio and Boulder Outline in the New and Old Worlds." *University of California Berkeley Archaeological Survey Reports.* 20:30.

[21]Clapp, Nicholas, 2015. *Old Magic: Lives of the Desert Shamans.* Sunbelt Publications, San Diego.

[22]Personal communication, Steve Lucas to Imperial Valley Desert Museum staff. February 2013.

[23]Lynch, John S., John W. Kennedy, and Robert L. Wooley, 1982. *Patton's Desert Training Center.* Council on America's Military Past, Fort Myer, Virginia. In 1942, General George S. Patton organized and commanded the Desert Training Center (DTC). This DTC was active for only thirteen months. In November 1943, the DTC was expanded and renamed the California-Arizona Maneuver Area (CAMA). This larger training area extended from Pomona, California, east for 350 miles to near Boulder City, Nevada. This extensive area offered ideal desert training conditions for infantry and armored units destined for desert combat areas. Twenty of the eighty-seven divisions trained in the Southwestern deserts.

[24]Jones, Terry L. and Kathryn A. Klar (editors), 2007. *California Prehistory: Colonization, Culture, and Complexity.* AltaMira Press, New York.

[25]Harner, Michael J., 1953. "Gravel Pictographs of the Lower Colorado River Region." *Reports of the University of California Archaeological Survey Papers on California Archaeology.* 21-22(20):1-32. University of California, Berkeley.

[26]Coppens, Philip, 2011. "America's Nazca Lines." *Philip Coppens.* http://www.philipcoppens.com/intaglios.htm. Accessed 16 August 2011.

[27]Story by the late Lee Emerson, informant from the Quechan tribe who lived near Yuma, Arizona. He also disclosed that the evil giant's name was Kwa-You.

[28]Waters, Frank, 1971. *Book of the Hopi.* Ballantine, New York: p. 87.

"The people liked this location so much that they again stopped here after they had traveled westward to the Pacific and back. This time they found evidence that the Fire Clan and the Water Clan also stopped to work the fertile bottom-lands, but had quarreled, and the Fire Clan had driven the Water Clan away. The story was told by one great figure on the ground, made of rocks. It was the figure of the Fire Clan Deity, arms outstretched to show the fire Clan had driven the Water Clan away and was barring its return."

[29]Bureau of Land Management, 2008. "Blythe Intaglios." *Bureau of Land Management Cultural and Historic Sites.* U.S. Department of the Interior Bureau of Land Management, 7 September 2008. https://web.archive.org/web/20080907020243/http://www.blm.gov/az/cultural/intaglios.htm. Accessed 6 September 2017.

[30]Clapp, Nicholas. *Old Magic.* p. 5.

[31]Ibid. p. 5.

[32]Waters. *Book of the Hopi.*

[33]Corbusier, William, 1886. "The Apache-Yumas and Apache-Mohaves." *American Antiquarian.* 8(6):325-339.

[34]Haenszel, Arda M., 1978. "Topock Maze: Commercial or Aboriginal?" *San Bernardino County Museum Association Quarterly.* 26(1):1-60.

[35]Richardson, Gary, 1976. "Armagosan Mystery Rings." *Desert Magazine.* January 1976: 12-15.

[36]Jones and Klar. *California Prehistory.*

[37]Ibid.

[38]Sitgreave, Lorenzo, 1962. *Report of an Expedition down the Zuni and the Colorado Rivers in 1851.* (First published 1853.) Rio Grande Press, Chicago.

[39]The discrepancy in the spelling of Kumastamo (Kumastamxo, Kumustamho, and Mustamho) is probably caused by variations in the pronunciations by the different groups and inconsistent translations by different ethnographers.

[40]Quechan Indian Museum display. Yuma, Arizona. On a wall of the museum was a hand-drawn likeness of the geoglyph, which bears the caption "Kumastamo makes the Colorado River flow by thrusting a spear into the ground." Near that illustration is another drawing of "Kustamo" that tells of his relationship to the Quechan. Noted by Harry Casey.

[41]"Colorado River Indian Tribes. http://www.crit-nsn.gov/crit_contents/tourism/http://cip.azlibrary.gov/Institution.aspx?InsID=123 (retrieved 2/4/15).

[42]Waters. *Book of the Hopi.* p. 124.

[43]Ibid. p. 124 "As the migration began to end, the record of the people's wanderings was left engraved on rocks over the face of all the land… In the migration symbols shown, the circles record the number of rounds or pasos covered, north, east, south, and west. The one at Oraibi shows they completed four circles, with three points covered on the return. The Chaco Canyon symbol indicates two points covered and that the people are returning, as the second circle moves in the opposite direction. The people at Gila Bend, Arizona, were on their third round when the symbol was inscribed, but stayed some time, as indicated by the connecting line. The clan signature is that of the snake. The square and circle both mean the same at Mesa Verde, Colorado."

[44]Russell, Frank, 1908. "The Pima Indians." *26th Annual Report of American Ethnology to the Secretary of the Smithsonian Institution.* 26th U.S. Govt. Print. Off., Washington: pp. 222–223. "The people wished to destroy the child, because it had long claws instead of fingers and toes; its teeth were long and sharp, like those of a dog. They gave it the name of Ha-ak, meaning something dreadful or ferocious. This female child grew to maturity in three or four years' time. She ate anything she could get her hands on, either raw or cooked food. The people tried to kill her, because she killed and ate their children. She went to the mountain Ta'-atukam and lived there for a while in a cave. Then she went to Baboquivari for a time and then to Poso Verde, where she was killed by Elder Brother…. When he killed Ha-ak a great feast was made, just as when Eagle was killed, and to this day the cave remains there where Ha-ak was killed, and 2 or 3 miles distant is a stone enclosure, Ha-ak moakkut, Place where Ha-ak was killed. The people formerly placed offerings within the enclosure to bring them good luck."

[45]Ibid, p. 254. "Ha-ak Va-ak, Ka-ak Lying, is a crude outline of a human figure situated about five miles north of Sacaton. It was made by scraping aside the small stones with which the mesa is there thickly strewn to form furrows about 50 cm. wide. The body furrow is 35 m. long and has a small heap of stones at the head, another at a distance of 11 m. long and 1 m. apart. The arms curve outward from the head and terminate in small pyramids. In all the piles of stone, which have a temporary and modern appearance, are glass beads and rages, together with fresh creosote branches, showing that the place is yet visited. The beads are very old and much weathered. Besides the large figure is a smaller one that is 4.5 m. long, the body being 2.7. Ha-ak is supposed to have slept one night at this place before reaching Ha-ak Teia Hak, a cave in the Ta-atukam mountains, where she remained for some time."

[46]In the Southern California deserts, more than 6,300 square miles are reserved for military activities. Likewise, in the desert area of southwestern Arizona, from the Colorado River east to Phoenix, then south to the Mexican border are restricted areas totaling more than 6,400 square miles.

[47]Möller, Harry and Ernesto L. Aguilar, 1982. "El Enigma de Machui." *Mexico Desconocido.* 66: 4-7.

REFERENCES

Arizona-Sonoran Desert Museum
n.d.   *Regional Natural History: The Sonoran Desert Region and Its Subdivisions.* Electronic document, Arizona-Sonoran Desert Museum. https://www.desertmuseum.org/desert/sonora.php. Accessed 6 September 2017.

Arnold, H.H.
1959   Who Drew These Giants Along the Colorado? *Westways* 51(10):20-21. Reprinted from *Touring Topics.* (24) 1932.

Aveni, Anthony F.
1986   The Nazca Lines: Patterns in the Desert. *Archaeology Magazine* 39(4):32-39.

Aveni, Anthony F. (editor)
1977   *Native American Astronomy.* University of Texas Press, Austin, Texas.

Bancroft-Hunt, Norman
1979   *People of the Totem.* Orbis Publishers, London, England.

Barnes, F. A.
1982   *Canyon Country Prehistoric Rock Art.* Wasatch Publishers Inc., Salt Lake City, Utah.

Bassett, Carol Ann
1986   Mystery of the Desert Giants. *American West Magazine* 23(2):30-37.

1989   The Desert's Mysterious Legacy: Lonely Giants. *Arizona Highways Magazine* 65(4):38-45.

Bear, Sun Wabun
1986   *The Medicine Wheel.* Prentice Hall Press, New York, New York.

Berndt, Ronald M. and Eric S. Phillips (editors)
1973   *The Australian Aboriginal Heritage.* Paul Hamlyn Pty Limited, Sydney, Australia.

Bowen, Thomas
1976   *Seri Prehistory: The Archaeology of the Central Coast of Sonora Mexico.* University of Arizona, Tucson, Arizona.

Bureau of Land Management
2008   *Blythe Intaglios.* Electronic document, Bureau of Land Management Cultural and Historic Sites. Accessed 7 September 2008. https://web.archive.org/web/20080907020243/http://www.blm.gov/az/cultural/intaglios.htm. Accessed 6 September 2017.

Burl, Aubrey
1979   *Rings of Stone.* Frances Lincoln Publishers Limited, London, England.

Burland, Cottie
1965   *North American Indian Mythology.* Hamlyn Publishing Group Limited, New York, NY.

Cerda, Pablo F., Sixto F. Fernandez, and Jaime V. Estay
1985   Prospecion de Geoglifos de la Provincia de Iquique, Primera Region Tarapaca, Norte de Chile: Informe Preliminar. *Estudios en Arte Rupestre Museu Chileno de Arte Precolombino,* 311-348.

Cerveny, Nicole Villa, Russell Kaldenberg, Judyth Reed, David S. Whitley, Joseph Simon, and Roanld I. Dorn
2006   A New Strategy for Analyzing the Chronometry of Constructed Rock Features in Deserts. *Geoarchaeology* 21(3):281-303.

Clapp, Nicholas
2015   *Old Magic: Lives of the Desert Shamans.* Sunbelt Publications, San Diego, California.

Coppens, Philip
　2011　America's Nazca Lines. Philip Coppens. http://www.philipcoppens.com/intaglios.html. 16 August 2011.

Corbusier, William
　1886　The Apache-Yumas and Apache-Mohaves. *American Antiquarian* 8(5):276-284.

　1886　The Apache-Yumas and Apache-Mohaves. *American Antiquarian* 8(6):325-339.

Davis, Emma Lou and Clark W. Brott
　1982　Shamanic Dreams and Drying Lakes. *Individual Abstract at the Society for California Archaeology.* San Diego California, March 24, 1982.

Davis, Emma L., Kathrun H. Brown, and Jacqueline Nichols
　1980　*Evaluation of Early Human Activities and Remains in the California Desert.* Great Basin Foundation, San Diego, California.

Davis, Emma Lou and Sylvia Winslow
　1965　Giant Ground Figures of the Prehistoric Deserts. *American Philosophical Society, Proceedings* (109):8-21.

Dorn, Ronald I.
　1991　Rock Varnish. *American Scientist* 79(6):542-553.

Dorn, Ronald I., Persis B. Clarkson, Margaret F. Nobbs, Lawrence L. Loendorf, and D.S. Whitley
　1992　New Approach to the Radiocarbon Dating of Rock Varnish with Examples from Drylands. *Annals of the Association of American Geographers* 82(1):136-151.

Eaton, Evelyn
　1989　*The Shaman and the Medicine Wheel.* Quest Books, Wheaton, Illinois.

Fernandez, Sixto Guillermo
　1987　Geoglyphs in the Iquique Province of Northern Chile. Excerpt from *Spirit of Enterprise: The 1987 Rolex Awards* 227-230. David W. Reed (ed). Van Nosttand Reinhold (UK) Co. Ltd., Wokingham, Berkshire, England.

Flood, Josephine
　1983　*Archaeology of the Dreamtime.* William Collins Pty, Ltd., Sydney, Australia.

Foster, Steven and Meredith Little
　1983　*Vision Quest.* Prentice Hall Press, New York.

Germani, Clara
　1983　Saving the Southwest's Mysterious Geoglyphs. *The Christian Science Monitor.* January 20, 1983:12-13.

Grant, Campbell
　1981　*Rock Art of the American Indian.* Outbooks, Golden, Colorado.

Gresser, Percy John
　1960　Stone Arrangements of the Aborigines of the Bathurst District. *Papers of Percy J. Gresser.* MS 21 (21/7). National Library of Australia. http://trove.nla.gov.au/version/9205037. Accessed September 2017.

Hadingham, Evan
　1987　*Lines to the Mountain Gods: Nazca and the Mysteries of Peru.* Random House, New York, New York.

Haenszel, Arda M.
　1978　Topock Maze: Commercial or Aboriginal? *San Bernardino County Museum Association Quarterly* 26(1):1-60.

　1981　Series of Ground Figures in Mohave Valley. *Archaeological Survey Association Journal* 5(1):20-25.

Harner, Michael J.
　1953　Gravel pictographs of the Lower Colorado River Region. *Reports of the University of California Archaeological Survey Papers on California Archaeology* 21-22(20):1-32. University of California, Berkeley, California.

　1980　*The Way of the Shaman.* Harper & Row Publishers, Inc., Toronto.

Hayden, Julian D.
　1982　Ground Figures of the Sierra Pinacate, Sonora, Mexico. In *Hohokan and Patayan: Prehistory of Southwestern Arizona.* Randal H. McGuire and Michael B. Schiffer (editors): pgs. 581-588. Academic Press, New York, New York.

Heizer, Robert F.
　1953　Additional Surface Intaglio and Boulder Outline in the New and Old Worlds. *University of California Berkeley Archaeological Survey Reports* 20:30-31.

Heizer, Robert F., and Martin Baumhoff
　1962　*Prehistoric Rock Art of Nevada and Eastern California.* University of California Press, Berkeley, California.

Heizer, Robert F., and Martin A. Whipple
1971   *The California Indians: A Source Book*. University of California Press, Berkeley, California.

Hightower, Jamake
1981   *The Primal Mind: Vision and Reality in Indian America*. Meridian Book/New America Library, New York, New York.

Hill, Ray, and Beth Hill
1975   *Indian Petroglyphs of the Pacific Northwest*. University of Washington Press, Seattle, Washington.

Houghton, Samuel G.
1976   *A Trace of Desert Waters: The Great Basin Story*. Howe Brothers, Chicago.

Hudson, Travis, Georgia Lee, and Ken Hedges
1979   Solstice Observers and Observations in Native California. *Journal of California and Great Basin Anthropology* 1(1):38-63.

Hunt, Charles B.
1975   *Death Valley: Geology-Ecology-Archaeology*. University of California Press, Los Angeles.

Huyghe, Rene
1962   *Larousse Encyclopedia of Prehistoric and Ancient Art*. Prometheus Press, New York, New York.

Isbell, William H.
1978   The Prehistoric Ground Drawings of Peru. *Scientific American* 239(4):140-153.

Jaeger, Edmund C.
1965   *The California Deserts*. Stanford University Press, Stanford, California.

Johnson, Boma
1981   *Geoglyphs Along the Lower Colorado River: A Research Prospectus*. Unpublished Manuscript. Bureau of Land Management, Yuma, Arizona.

1985   *Earth Figures of the Lower Colorado and Gila River Deserts: A Functional Analysis*. Arizona Archaeological Society, Yuma, Arizona.

Jones, Frederick Wood
1925   The Ordered Arrangement of Stones Present in Certain Parts of Australia. *Royal Anthropological Institute Journal* 55(Jan.-Jun.):123-128.

Jones, Terry L. and Kathryn A. Klar (editors)
2007   *California Prehistory: Colonization, Culture, and Complexity*. AltaMira Press, New York.

Kroeber, Alfred L.
1976   *Handbook of the Indians of California*. Dover Publications, New York. Originally published in *Bulletin 78 of the Bureau of American Ethnology of the Smithsonian Institution* (Washington, D.C.: Government Printing Office, 1923).

Lynch, John S., John W. Kennedy, and Robert L. Wooley
1982   *Patton's Desert Training Center*. Council on America's Military Past, Fort Myer, Virginia.

MacKnight, Campbell C. and W.J. Gray
1970   Aboriginal Stone Pictures in Eastern Arhem Land. *Australian Institute of Aboriginal Studies, Prehistory and Material Culture Series* 27(6):1-44.

Marshack, Alexander
1985   Theoretical Concepts that Lead to New Analytic Methods, Modes of Inquirey and Classes of Data. *Rock Art Research: The Journal of the Australian Rock Art Research Association* 2(2):95-105.

McBrydey, Isabel
1963   An Unusual Series of Stone Arrangements Near the Serpentine River, Eber District, New South Wales. *Oceania* 34(2):137-146.

McCarthey, Frederick D.
1940   Aboriginal Stone Arrangements in Australia. *Australian Museum Magazine* 7(5):184-189.

McGuire, Randall H. and Michael B. Schiffer (editors)
1982   *Hohokam and Patayan: Prehistory of Southwestern Arizona*. Academic Press, New York, New York.

McIntyre, Loren
1975   Mystery of the Nazca Lines. *National Geographic* 148(5):716-728.

Möller, Harry and Ernesto L. Aguilar
1982   El Enigma de Machui. *Mexico Desconocido* 66:4-7.

National Oceanic and Atmospheric Administration
2011   Mid-Holocene Warm Period—About 6,000 Years Ago. *National Oceanic and Atmospheric Administration*. https://www.ncdc.noaa.gov/global-warming/mid-holocene-warm-period. Accessed 3 November 2017.

Palmer, Kingsely
1977   Stone Arrangements and Mythology. *Mankind* 11(1):33-38.

Pfeiffer, John E.
1982   *The Creative Explosion*, Cornell University Press, New York, New York.

Richardson, Gary
1976   Armagosan Mystery Rings. *Desert Magazine.* January 1976:12-15.

Rogers, Malcolm
1973   *Early Lithic Industries of the Lower Basin of the Colorado River and Adjacent Desert Areas.* Bellena Press, San Diego, California.

Russell, Frank
1908   The Pima Indians. *26th Annual Report of American Ethnology to the Secretary of the Smithsonian Institution.* 26th U.S. Govt. Print. Office, Washington, D.C.

Salton Sea Authority
1997   *The Salton Sea: A Brief Description of Its Condition and Potential Remediation Projects.* The Salton Sea Authority. October 3, 1997 *SDSU* Center for Inland Waters Salton Basin-Colorado Delta. www.sci.sdsu.edu/salton/Salton%20Sea%20Description.html. Accessed September 7, 2017.

Schultes, Richard Evans and Albert Hoffman
1987   *Plants of the Gods: Origins of Hallucinogenic Use.* A. van der Marck Editions, New York, New York.

Selzer, Frank M.
1952   Seeking the Secret of the Giants. *National Geographic Magazine* 102(3):390-404.

Silverberg, Robert
1989   *The Mound Builders.* Ohio University Press, Athens, Ohio.

Sitgreave, Lorenzo
1962   *Report of an Expedition down the Zuni and the Colorado Rivers in 1851.* (First published 1853.) Rio Grande Press, Chicago. Originally published as *Executive Document 59 United States Senate.* Washington, D.C.

Smith, Gerald A.
1974   *Investigations of Known Intaglios Located Along the Colorado River Between Ripley and Old Fort Mohave.* Unpublished manuscript, Bureau of Land Management, Yuma, Arizona.

Smith, Gerald A. and Wilson G. Turner
1975   *Indian Rock Art of Southern California.* San Bernardino County Museum, San Bernadino, California.

Solari, Elain Maryse and Boma Johnson
1982   Intaglios: A Syntheses of Known Information and Recommendations for Management. *Hohokam and Patayan: Prehistory of the Southwestern Arizona.* R.H. McGuire and M.B. Schiffer (eds). Pgs. 417-432, Academic Press, New York, New York.

Spencer, Paul
1985   *Society and the Dance.* Cambridge University Press, Cambridge, England.

Spencer, Robert and Jesse D. Jennings (editors)
1977   *The Native Americans*, 2nd edition. Harper and Row, New York, New York.

Spier, Leslie
1970   *Yuma Tribes of the Gila River.* Cooper Square Publishers, New York, New York.

Swan, James A.
1990   *Sacred Places.* Bear and Company Publications, Rochester, Vermont.

VandenDolder, Evelyn M.
1992   Rock Varnish and Desert Pavement Provide Geological and Archaeological Records. *Arizona Geology* 22(1):1-9.

Van Tilburg, Jo Anne (editor)
1983   *Ancient Images on Stone.* UCLA Rock Art Archives, Los Angeles, California.

Von Werlhof, Jay
1958   Granite Galleries. *Pacific Discovery* 11(4):149-156.

1987   *Spirits of the Earth, Volume 1: The Northern Desert.* Imperial Valley College Desert Museum, El Centro, California.

1999   E=MC^2: Implications of Power in Yuha Desert Geoglyphs. *Rock Art Papers*, Volume 14. Ken Hedges (editor). San Diego Museum of Man, San Diego, California.

2004   *That They May Know and Remember, Volume 2: Spirits of the Earth.* Imperial Valley College Desert Museum Society, El Centro, California.

Von Werlhof, Jay, Harry Casey, Ronald I. Dorn, and Glenn A. Jones
1995   AMS ^{14}C Age Constraints and Geoglyphs in the Lower Colorado River Region. *Geoarchaeology: An International Journal* 10(4):257-275.

Von Werlhof, Jay, Casey Nopah, and Welton Johnson
  1982 *Two Worlds of Archaeology: A Case Study.* Paper presented to the Society for California Archaeology, Sacramento, California: April 2, 1982.

Waisbard, Simone
  1981 Enigmatic Messages of the Nazcas. The World's Last Mysteries. *Reader's Digest* (editors): 281-287. Reader's Digest Association, New York, New York.

Wallace, Noel Malcolm
  1980 Western Desert Rock and Stone Arrangements. *Artefact* 5(3/4):111-122.

Waters, Frank
  1971 *Book of the Hopi.* Ballantine, New York, New York.

Waters, Michael R.
  1983 Late Holocene Lacustrine Chronology and Archaeology of Ancient Lake Cahuilla, California. *Quarternary Research* 19(3):373-387.

RECOMMENDED READING

Baja's Wild Side: A Photographic Journey Through Baja California's Pacific Coast Region
Daniel Cartamil, Ph. D.
Baja's Wild Side features the photography and stories of shark biologist Dr. Daniel Cartamil, as he explores Baja California's Pacific coast region.

Cave Paintings of Baja California: Discovering the Great Murals of an Unknown People
Harry W. Crosby
Central Baja hosts one of the five greatest sites in the world for the Great Mural style and ranks with those of the Pyrenees, northwest Africa, and outback Australia. These ancient giant, ghostly figures are only accessible by arduous days-long trekking with local guides or this lavishly illustrated full-color account.

Chasing Centuries: The Search for Ancient Agave Cultivars Across the Desert Southwest
Ron Parker
Chasing Centuries is a one-of-a-kind travel-history book that takes the reader on an exciting adventure at the crossroads of archaeology and botany. Discover interesting assortments of agaves associated with sites abandoned by residents of extinct ancient cultures. These agaves appear to be living relics developed and planted by pre-Columbian Native Americans; still growing where they were planted hundreds of years ago.

Dreamers of the Colorado: Their Land and Religion Part 1

Dreamers of the Colorado: Their Culture and Arts Part 2
Frances L. O'Neil and Paul W. Wittmer, eds.
These two volumes are a fascinating collection of true accounts dealing with the history, culture, art and religion of the Mojave Indians. While reading about them, you will experience the actual life of the people. Many elders have passed away. Hear their words in this book and go on a journey with them in the land of the Mojave Indians.

Earth Pigments and Paint of the California Indians
Paul Douglas Campbell
Hundreds of rare photographs parallel this scholarly but accessible text on the cave paintings and body paint of California's Indians. Full-color photos depict an array of artifacts and images.

Fossil Treasures of the Anza-Borrego Desert
George T. Jefferson, Lowell Lindsay, Eds.
A richly illustrated volume by 23 leading scientists and specialists that reveals North America's most continuous fossil record for the last 7 million years. Includes camels, giant sloths, mammoths, and sabertooth cats.

Old Magic: Lives of the Desert Shamans
Nicholas Clapp
Drawing on the lore of a dozen tribes, Old Magic reveals the life of a shaman—a life of service to his people, a life fraught with torment and danger.

Rock Art of the Grand Canyon Region
D. Christensen, J. Dickey, & S. Freers
This visually stunning book opens a window to the past within this majestic region rarely seen by the millions of visitors who visit this area annually. It is a feast to both the serious rock art researcher and to the general public who may not be aware of the enticing and elaborately rich rock art found in some of the more remote areas within this spectacular landscape.

The Universal Tool Kit: Out of Africa to Native California
Paul Douglas Campbell
From earliest Stone Age in Africa to 20th century California, our ancestors used rocks and bones to make tools. They comprised most important survival kit ever invented, it altered the very shape of the human species and for millions of years was truly a universal tool kit.